STUDIES IN ECONOMIC AND SOCIAL HISTORY

This series, specially commissioned by the Economic History
Society, provides a guide to the current interpretations of the
key them

have rece

debate.

Origina

series had

and the

History',

The se

them to

and by n

them in t

springbo

conclusio

ECONO

The Eco

members

year (fre

Enquirie

Assistant

Cambrid

rates.

STUDIES IN ECONOMIC AND SOCIAL HISTORY

Edited for the Economic History Society by T. C. Smout

PUBLISHED

Bill Albert Latin America and the World Economy from Independence to 1930
B. W. E. Alford Depression and Recovery? British Economic Growth, 1918–1939
Michael Anderson Approaches to the History of the Western Family, 1500–1914
P. J. Cain Economic Foundations of British Overseas Expansion, 1815–1914
S. D. Chapman The Cotton Industry in the Industrial Revolution
Neil Charlesworth British Rule and the Indian Economy, 1800–1914
J. A. Chartres Internal Trade in England, 1500–1700
R. A. Church The Great Victorian Boom, 1850–1873
D. C. Coleman Industry in Tudor and Stuart England
P. L. Cottrell British Overseas Investment in the Nineteenth Century
Ralph Davis English Overseas Trade, 1500–1700
M. E. Falkus The Industrialisation of Russia, 1700–1914
Peter Fearon The Origins and Nature of the Great Slump, 1929–1932
T. R. Gourvish Railways and the British Economy, 1830–1914
Robert Gray The Aristocracy of Labour in Nineteenth-century Britain, *c.* 1850–1900
John Hatcher Plague, Population and the English Economy, 1348–1530
J. R. Hay The Origins of the Liberal Welfare Reforms, 1906–1914
R. H. Hilton The Decline of Serfdom in Medieval England
E. L. Jones The Development of English Agriculture, 1815–1873
John Lovell British Trade Unions, 1875–1933
J. D. Marshall The Old Poor Law, 1795–1834
Alan S. Milward The Economic Effects of the Two World Wars on Britain
G. E. Mingay Enclosure and the Small Farmer in the Age of the Industrial Revolution
Rosalind Mitchison British Population Change Since 1860
R. J. Morris Class and Class Consciousness in the Industrial Revolution, 1780–1850
J. Forbes Munro Britain in Tropical Africa, 1880–1960
A. E. Musson British Trade Unions, 1800–1875
R. B. Outhwaite Inflation in Tudor and Early Stuart England
R. J. Overy The Nazi Economic Recovery, 1932–1938
P. L. Payne British Entrepreneurship in the Nineteenth Century
G. D. Ramsay The English Woollen Industry, 1500–1750
Michael E. Rose The Relief of Poverty, 1834–1914
Michael Sanderson Education, Economic Change and Society in England, 1780–1870
S. B. Saul The Myth of the Great Depression, 1873–1896
Arthur J. Taylor Laissez-faire and State Intervention in Nineteenth-century Britain
Peter Temin Causal Factors in American Economic Growth in the Nineteenth Century
Michael Turner Enclosures in Britain, 1750–1830
Margaret Walsh The American Frontier Revisited

OTHER TITLES ARE IN PREPARATION

The Economic Effects of the Two World Wars on Britain

Second Edition

Prepared for
The Economic History Society by

ALAN S. MILWARD

Professor of European Studies
University of Manchester Institute of
Science and Technology
and
Professor of Contemporary History
European University Institute

MACMILLAN

First edition 1972
Second edition 1984

Published by
. Higher and Further Education Division
MACMILLAN PUBLISHERS LTD
*London and Basingstoke
Companies and representatives
throughout the world*

*Typeset by
Wessex Typesetters Ltd
Frome, Somerset*

Printed in Hong Kong

British Library Cataloguing in Publication Data
Milward, Alan
The economic effects of the two world wars on
Britain.—2nd ed.—(Studies in economic and
social history)
1. Great Britain—Economic conditions—1918–1945
I. Title   II. Series
330.941′083   HC256.8
ISBN 0–333–36954–8

Contents

Acknowledgements

A work of this kind cannot pretend to any originality, but the form which it took persuaded me how much it owed to my former colleagues, the late Professor M. W. Flinn, Professor T. C. Smout and Professor S. B. Saul. When I had written it it seemed only right that they should read it. They all very kindly did so, thereby making it even more their own work.

Note to the Second Edition

Over the thirteen years since the publication of the first edition scholars have continued to discuss the subject of this book and, particularly in regard to the First World War, have added substantially to the literature on it. More significantly, the focus of interest has changed with the marked changes in the British economy and the international position of the country. This has meant not merely a revision of the existing text but the production of what is virtually a completely new book, no matter how closely it adheres to the pattern of the first edition.

Note on References·

References in the text within square brackets relate to the numbered items in the Select Bibliography, followed, where necessary, by the page numbers in italic, for example: [5:27].

Editor's Preface

SINCE 1968, when the Economic History Society and Macmillan published the first of the 'Studies in Economic and Social History', the series has established itself as a major teaching tool in universities, colleges and schools, and as a familiar landmark in serious bookshops throughout the country. A great deal of the credit for this must go to the wise leadership of its first editor, Professor M. W. Flinn, who retired at the end of 1977. The books tend to be bigger now than they were originally, and inevitably more expensive; but they have continued to provide information in modest compass at a reasonable price by the standards of modern academic publications.

There is no intention of departing from the principles of the first decade. Each book aims to survey findings and discussion in an important field of economic or social history that has been the subject of recent lively debate. It is meant as an introduction for readers who are not themselves professional researchers but who want to know what the discussion is all about – students, teachers and others generally interested in the subject. The authors, rather than either taking a strongly partisan line or suppressing their own critical faculties, set out the arguments and the problems as fairly as they can, and attempt a critical summary and explanation of them from their own judgement. The discipline now embraces so wide a field in the study of the human past that it would be inappropriate for each book to follow an identical plan, but all volumes will normally contain an extensive descriptive bibliography.

The series is not meant to provide all the answers but to help readers to see the problems clearly enough to form their own conclusions. We shall never agree in history, but the discipline will be well served if we know what we are disagreeing about, and why.

T. C. SMOUT

University of Edinburgh Editor

The Subject

IN the history of the United Kingdom in this century the two world wars have been so terrible a reality that historians have related to them, directly or indirectly, an astonishing number of developments. The difference in economic organisation and in social life between wartime and peacetime has been so huge and so encapsulated in the personal consciousness of so many still alive that the wish to produce a comprehensive theory of the relationship between war and history starts from the soil turned by even the most aridly factual of labourers. It is to these theories as they relate to the history of the British economy in this century that this pamphlet is directed. What changes in the economy have historians and economists laid to the account of the two world wars? And what changes may justly so be laid?

At the outset appears a methodological problem of no great complexity. So great was the economic effort needed to win both wars that while those wars were being fought, and under the pressure of fighting them, on each occasion the economy was quite transformed from what it had been in peacetime. The aim was to win, for most of the Second World War to win no matter what the cost. Therefore the main economic priority was to produce the necessary quantity of goods to defeat the enemy. Consequently the ultimate economic purpose was quite different from that of peacetime, and the kind of economy which was created has come to be known loosely by the term 'war economy'. The term is a loose one, for it is a matter of historical fact that most of the 'war economies' which have existed have neither had such simple priorities as, nor much resemblance to, the war economies which existed in Britain. It may even be questioned whether historians have not exaggerated the degree of unanimity of purpose which informed the economy in Britain during the two world wars. Nevertheless it must be stated that it is a matter of almost universal agreement that the British nation twice bent its united energies to creating an economy whose dominating purpose was to defeat the enemy, sweeping aside, gradually in the First World War, and almost from the beginning in the Second, most other claims on that economy.

The result of this apparent clarity of purpose was to create a form of economic organisation for the duration of the war which was sharply different from that of the preceding and succeeding periods of peace. Those changes in the economy and in society which did not endure, the short-term changes, will not concern us very much here. They are not the subject of controversy except in their more minute details. Indeed they have been described in such detail, with government help, for the Second World War so effectively as to stop all but the most interested of historians from considering them at all. There are many perfectly adequate summaries in textbooks and the like of what the short-term changes in the economy were.[1] We may therefore resolve our methodological difficulty by concentrating on the more controversial problem of the long-term changes in the economy and society brought about by war in this century, considering the short-term changes only when necessary and in this wider context.

It is as well that we should be able so to simplify the issue. For the opinions about these long-term trends are often vague, differing enormously in their ultimate implications, but sometimes having a quite misleading resemblance to each other. The differences between them reflect the changes in British society, and in the way we have come to think about that society, over the last seventy years. For that reason they are considered first in roughly chronological order. They represent a set of changing concepts, each concept a framework wherein the actual historical events and economic facts may be fitted more or less successfully.

Its Changing Interpretation

FROM the second quarter of the eighteenth century economists evolved the idea that war was an almost unmitigated economic disaster. By the end of the century that view had become almost generally established and, excepting the notable dissent of Malthus, it remained more or less unchanged in Britain until the outbreak of the First World War. The earliest writers to consider the impact of that war on the economy took, therefore, an unrelievedly gloomy view of its results. They would have echoed what was already becoming received opinion when Samuel Johnson published, in 1749, his imitation of Juvenal's tenth Satire:

> Yet Reason frowns on War's unequal Game,
> Where wasted Nations raise a single Name,
> And mortgag'd States their Grandsires' Wreaths regret,
> From Age to Age in everlasting Debt.[2]

Many of them did indeed afterwards echo this idea almost exactly. 'Thus the Great War', wrote Hirst and Allen in 1928, 'brought a load of debt, taxes and misery incalculable. The expenditure during the four years that it lasted reached a total incomprehensible and inconceivable to the ordinary mind'. [32: *18*].

This interpretation, which we may call the classical liberal interpretation, saw war in relatively simple terms as a loss. However complex the event, the net result was always a loss to the economy, of cash, of production, of capital and of people. R. H. Brand, himself a merchant banker, summarised this view in the series of analyses of government policy which he published throughout the First World War. 'They were not able to see that all this outpouring of our substance on the war was accompanied by a constant deterioration of our economic situation, by a vast loss of national capital, and by the creation of a huge load of debt, internal and external – in fact that we were like a spendthrift, living more or less at our ease by wasting our capital' [9: *256*]. Although, he conceded, war on such a scale as the First World War represented an immense productive effort, what was produced was essentially 'non-productive wealth'. Meanwhile 'productive wealth' was being destroyed and capital allowed to depreciate. The inflation accompanying the war with its effect on money wages and national income was only disguising the fact that in the long run the country's productive capacity and purchasing power were being steadily reduced to the point where a depression would certainly be produced after the war. When that depression did arrive in 1920, Brand, and others who shared his standpoint, therefore blamed it on the war. That the depression of the 1920s was to be blamed directly or indirectly on the First World War was all too easy a deduction from the theoretical assumptions underlying this view of war. Lloyd George, introducing the first budget of the war, prophesied a brief period of prosperity at the end of the war followed by a severe industrial crisis. The most ardent, although not the most profound, advocate of this well-established interpretation was F. W. Hirst, whose book, *The Consequences of the War to Great Britain*, was published in 1934. He also categorised the depression of 1920 as being the 'automatic' result of the war, aggravated by the foolish policy pursued by the government of not raising a sufficient proportion of the war expenditure by higher taxation. Greater taxation would have meant less borrowing, less borrowing would have meant a less crippling public debt in the 1920s. 'The expenses of a war', said Gladstone, introducing the Crimean war budget to the House of Commons, 'are the moral check which it has pleased the Almighty to impose upon the ambition and the lust of conquest that are inherent in so many nations.' This, however, did not absolve the public from the duty to suffer the same moral chastisement when resisting an aggressor. The consequence of their refusal in 1914–18, Hirst argued, was a burden of debt payments under which the 1920s foundered [33].

Since war was a loss, the best way its effects on the economy could be finally expressed was to calculate that loss as accurately as possible. Hirst and other writers sharing his liberal viewpoint therefore tried to add together the various elements of that loss and to 'cost' them. The effects of the First World War in their eyes could be expressed as what it had 'cost' the economy, or what sum of money would be sufficient to restore the economy to its previous state were that possible. However, whereas some elements of the total loss could be valued reasonably accurately without great difficulty, such as the value of the ships sunk and the cargo they contained, other elements were more elusive. The actual sum of money needed to pay for the war proved difficult to determine, and it was this problem which led Bogart, following the same interpretation as Hirst, to the notion that the total loss to the economy was compounded both of 'direct' and 'indirect' costs [6].

The 'direct costs' comprised the physical destruction of capital due to enemy action. For Britain a considerable part of this was the loss of armaments and shipping, the damage to capital within the national frontier being very small. But at this stage of evaluation the knotty question arose of how to value the human capital destroyed by enemy action. The liberal writers were perfectly justified in facing up to this question in the way they did, even though to our eyes their proceedings may suggest a certain heartlessness, for within the concept of 'direct costs' the loss of people was so obvious a fact that it could not be dodged. From the outbreak of war to its close the British Army and Navy lost at least 616,382 men, excluding those of colonial or dominion nationality, through enemy action or other forms of death. Over the same period 1,656,735 men were wounded, some of them so seriously that they would never be able to work again. Most of these people were in the prime of their working life and the proportion of officers killed and wounded was higher than that of men.

In developing the concept of 'human capital' Bogart and Hirst opened up a fertile field of economic enquiry but it was to prove more fruitful in other directions than in measuring the effect of the war.[3] Those killed or maimed in the First World War in Britain were far from a homogeneous group and when it is considered that conscription operated mainly on the basis of age and fitness the problems of determining the average capital value of a dead soldier will readily be seen. The values on which Bogart and Hirst finally settled were arbitrary. They attributed an average *per capita* value to the citizens of various belligerent countries.[4] That is to say that a dead American soldier was a much greater loss to the economy than a dead Serbian soldier, since not only was he a piece of human capital who had been much more expensive to educate and train to the moment of his death, but his subsequent productive capacity, had he not died,

12

would have been much greater. Bogart estimated the *per capita* value of a dead British soldier at $1,414, or $260 more than a dead German soldier, or more than twice the value of a dead Russian soldier. The elements in the calculation were the length of time the soldier would have been likely to live, the potential value of his lost labour, or the value of his potential savings plus his potential purchasing power plus his potential taxable capacity, and the cost to the state of supporting his family after his death or maiming.[5] The differences in value represent roughly the differences in the level of economic development of the countries concerned, the general conclusion being that in this respect the effect of the war on a highly developed country such as Britain was much more serious than on an underdeveloped country.

To accept this method of procedure it is necessary to accept a number of hypotheses. These are, that it is possible to calculate an average duration of life which is valid for all, that it is possible to calculate a potential average net income of those killed or maimed which would embrace the very wide differences in social class which existed in the British armed forces, and that it is possible to calculate an average potential consumption and express it in monetary terms. Nor will the critic be slow to indicate that national product *per capita* is not the same as the income received by the population. Nor can it be argued that the 'cost' to the economy can be shown if the casualty's potential consumption be deducted from his potential production, for it is only true that the loss of a man equals a certain reduction in national product if there is full employment and if the conditions of work remain the same for the time span of the calculation, that is to say until he would have died naturally. Had he been unemployed before the war the economy might actually have gained by his death, and there is little likelihood that, in whatever sector of production he had been employed, the production function in that sector would have remained unchanged for a further thirty years. Indeed, he would have been more likely to have been unemployed after the war. In addition there are the doubts cast on the procedure by demographic studies. Although so little comparative work on the demographic effects of war has been done that it is difficult

13

to generalise, the birth-rate immediately after the war appears to leap sharply, although temporarily, upwards [20]. Furthermore, in both wars there was a fall in infant mortality rates. And it is also possible that the wars produced a better standard of nutrition and health among the poorer classes, such that the beneficial effects of a healthier generation of children were then reproduced in successive demographic cycles [70]. There is evidence that, in this respect at least, the demographic 'loss' was not as great as might be assumed.

Of course, many of these methodological problems of evaluating the loss of human capital occur in attempting the same exercise for other parts of the capital stock destroyed. Much of it, like the people, might have been surplus to capacity in the economic conditions of the 1920s. By blaming these conditions on the debts accumulated during the war the liberal school avoided this awkward question by assuming, falsely, that it was tautological. To the relationship between post-war conditions and the events of the war itself we shall return in the last section of this pamphlet, where it will be seen that the question is much more complex than Bogart or Hirst assumed.

There is also a further difficulty which applies equally to the measurement of the 'indirect costs'. The relative value of the major currencies, which had remained more or less tied to each other for a long period, began to fluctuate wildly after 1914, so that no country's currency had the same purchasing power in 1918 as in 1914 and none retained the same relation to another. The unit of currency was therefore a rather unsatisfactory medium in which to evaluate the 'cost' of the war. In calculating 'indirect costs' Bogart's object was to arrive at a total of 'war expenses'. The sums of money officially allocated in 'war budgets' or raised by 'war loans' might not, however, effectively be spent purely on the prosecution of the war. Some part of the total might also serve as post-war investment. In any case the extension of the power of the government over economic life in directing the 'war economy' of the First World War was so great that the whole scope and purpose of the budget changed in those years. Bogart therefore calculated an average annual level of peacetime expenditure and deducted this for five years from the actual expenditure in the First World War, thus expressing the war expenses as $44,029,000,000.

It is easy to see the weaknesses in this method of procedure. Do the expenses of a war really begin with the declaration of war? And do they end when the fighting stops? What are 'normal' budgetary expenses? Jèze, who performed similar calculations for France, considered the 'war expenses' to be the difference in the public debt between the beginning and the end of war.[6] But the same questions must apply, apart from a further question about the size of the external debt. However, we are not so concerned here with those weaknesses as with the assumptions that fathered them. The nature of these assumptions can be simply revealed by posing a question that any economist would now pose. Is the extra expenditure entailed by war wholly a loss to the economy, or is some part of it actually beneficial in so far as it generates income by stimulating new employment and production?

Yet the assumptions which underlay the classical liberal interpretation were the current intellectual coin not only of historians but of those who made policy. Although in such a war as the First World War it was inevitable that the government could not raise the whole 'cost' of the war from taxation but had to borrow money, the Chancellor of the Exchequer, McKenna, applied to this borrowing policy the rule which came to be known as the 'McKenna rule', not to borrow without imposing new taxation sufficient to provide for the interest on, and a sinking fund to reduce, the new loans. More serious than this, the whole idea of the 'cost' of war was embodied in the demand for reparations from Germany. And this demand, embodied in government policy throughout the 1920s, created such international economic havoc as to be one of the main and most disastrous consequences of the war itself.

The domestic events of the First World War led many of those who were involved in them or who later studied them to question this concept of war as merely a 'cost' to the economy. In the first place there was the example of the United States. Even if the cost of the dead servicemen added to the cost of the sunk merchant ships and that of the supposedly lost foreign

15

trade was computed in the most generous fashion it was less than the upward movement in the value of industrial output over the same period. In Britain, too, in spite of the addition of five and a half million men to the armed forces at very low pay, national income per head after a steep drop in the first year of the war, increased from 1915 to 1918. In the Second World War it was to increase very steeply; in current prices it was 39 per cent higher in 1943 than its 1939 level, in real terms an increase of more than a quarter. Measured in this way the First World War represented a cyclical downturn followed by a vigorous upturn, the Second World War a vigorous and continuous boom the equal of any of the nineteenth-century booms.

The driving force of the boom was the war; 54 per cent of the national income in 1944 was spent on the war effort whereas in 1939 only 15 per cent had been spent on rearmament and war. What was 'lost' in certain sectors was more than replaced by much higher levels of output and employment in manufacturing industry (although by no means in *all* sectors of manufacturing industry) and by much higher levels of income and output in agriculture. During the First World War, in the absence of any overall concept of national income accounting these economic phenomena were observed only as isolated instances of prosperity in what was thought of as a world of sacrifice and it was these isolated and unsystematic observations which gave rise to so much hostile agitation and propaganda against 'war profiteers'. In the Second World War the idea that the war might, in fact, be paid for out of the increase in national income which it engendered became the guiding light of policy. So quickly did ideas change!

However, the strict liberal concepts of Hirst or Bogart were not always slavishly accepted by governments even before 1914 when it came to vital questions of national defence and during the First World War certain social and administrative phenomena gave rise to the idea that war was not an entirely negative experience and in doing so brought the wholly pessimistic economic interpretation of war into question. The full-time employment of a large part of the male population of whom few had previously experienced so long a period of regular employment at relatively high wages, the increase of about 1.6 million in the number of women brought into full-time employment, as well as the involvement of the civilian population in the war by aerial bombardment, by unrestricted submarine warfare against food supplies, by the enormous increase in employment in armaments industries, and by the impact of conscription on family life, all acted to change the kind of emotional involvement with war and its economic mechanisms. No longer were civilians hurrahing spectators; they became, like combatants, people who must be motivated by some clearly perceived objective to the struggle. There had to be a moral purpose. The administrative skills which geared the economy to allowing what had previously been thought of only as an economic waste to continue for so long, began now to be thought of as a means of achieving the moral purpose. For many, the purpose of the war became 'a better society' and if that required the economy to function differently from before 1914, it began to be argued, especially by those who had been involved in the remarkable administrative successes of the war effort, that this was essentially an administrative problem which could be solved and that, if politicians and administrators would will it, a better society could be created.

It is hardly surprising that under the conjoint pressures of a highly-charged emotional response and rapid and visible social change the views of economists and historians about war began to change. The change was one aspect of the growing interest in groups and in society as a whole rather than in individuals, but in this movement away from the mechanical accounting of Bogart to a concern with less strictly defined aspects of the human condition the experience of the First World War played a major role. By 1917, as feats of industrial output which would have been considered impossible before 1914 still allowed the immense and pitiful armies of foot-soldiers to be hurled at each other through the mud and débris of northern France, the war was coming to be seen not as a struggle between specialised fighting forces but as a 'total' war of one society against another, testing the very fabric of those societies at their weakest points.

The first steps towards this more sophisticated interpretation of the relationship between the economy, society and war were taken in the work of A. L. Bowley [7; 8]. His careful statistical analyses of the effects of the First World War have stood historians in good stead ever since. They are a fine example of the superiority of research over opinion, for in his general opinions Bowley differed scarcely a jot from Hirst, although his work repeatedly pointed the way to a widening of Hirst's views. He was convinced that 'whoever wins on the field, both sides lose in wealth' [8: *31*]. The size of the loss as far as Britain was concerned he put at between two and four years' normal accumulation of capital. He attributed the low level of employment in the 1920s to the scarcity of capital brought about by its destruction and depreciation in the war. The other long-term effects of the war which he was able to demonstrate proved the starting-point of much discussion. He agreed that the expenses of the war had resulted in a much greater burden of taxation, but demonstrated that the cumulative effect of this taxation was to redistribute a certain amount of income from the richer to the poorer. Taken together with the high level of employment during the war, the long hours and the high wages, and even when all allowance had been made for the wretched pittance paid to the soldiers, the net result was a narrowing of the gap between the poorer classes and the richer.

Bowley also drew attention to the technological consequences of the war for industry and society as a whole. Even during the war itself for many of those engaged in organising the supply of equipment to the armed forces the war had seemed to represent a miracle of production brought about by remarkable changes in technology and its application. The most striking example was perhaps the advances in aircraft manufacture. An industry which had scarcely existed before 1914 developed into a major mass-producing industrial sector. The consequences of this for civil life were not noticeable on any scale until after the Second World War which saw a great and lasting revival of the aircraft industry. But the development of radio, leading to the mass production after 1918 of the household receiving set, had a more immediate impact on civilian existence. So, too, did the numerous advances in production and managerial techniques, especially those of serial production, which the high levels of demand for certain goods and the tight labour market encouraged.

Lastly, Bowley drew attention to the social changes brought about by the war. Not only had the war reduced the gap between the classes and even brought into existence a system of taxation the effect of whose operations would be to continue to reduce that gap, but its events, and the involvement of so large a part of the population in them, had changed the general outlook of society. They had provided a perception of another system. 'The economic position of women and their more complete enfranchisement and independence with its multiform consequence, would no doubt have developed in a different manner if their claims had not been substantiated by their ability to replace men. In a somewhat similar way the services of all ranks in the Army and Navy, and the more general intermixture of classes, stimulated the sentiment of democracy and led to a more serious realisation of possibly avoidable economic inequalities and hardships, thus paving the way for the development of the insurance schemes and of more socialistic legislation' [8: 22].

As that enormous enterprise, the Carnegie Economic and Social History of the First World War, began to appear, many of the phenomena to which Bowley had drawn attention received further emphasis, but from a somewhat different point of view. Several of the volumes were written by wartime administrators and they were frequently concerned to explore the connections between government intervention in the economy, the development of direct economic controls and the social and economic changes which Bowley had observed. This was the case for example with the volumes by Beveridge and Lloyd [4; 42]. The production 'miracles' during the war were in fact primarily the result of the control and diversion of resources by the central government. Indeed, in the case of munitions they were the outcome of a specially created Ministry of Munitions with remarkable legal powers and at first a large degree of financial independence from the Treasury. Its powers extended across the whole field of industrial production and raw materials control and allocation. The changes in the fiscal system also depended, of course, on a change of purpose by central government. Employment too became the responsibility of a special ministry, and eventually a system of national food control and rationing was imposed over the most important foodstuffs in daily consumption.

The extension of government control was only a pragmatic response to the unforeseen stresses on the economy produced by a change of strategic plan. Many of the more successful administrators, Lord Rhondda, the Food Controller, or Beveridge, for instance, were dyed-in-the-wool liberals. The problems which they were called upon to solve began to present themselves as soon as the idea of fighting only a naval and amphibious campaign was abandoned and the army allowed to recruit a million new men between September and December 1914 [13; 25]. Even the smallest pragmatic acts of intervention turned out to have world-wide ramifications. The classic example is given by Lloyd [42]. The change in military tactics towards trench warfare at once produced a massive increase in the price of jute sacking, the material out of which the kilometres of sandbags stretching across northern France were made. Government intervention to force down the price immediately had a serious impact on the main supplier of jute fibre, India, whose economy had played a pivotal role in the pre-war network of international payments. Similarly, controlling the food supply meant controlling the purchase of imports from all over the world as well as the shipping in which they were carried and revealed at once the interconnections between levels of consumption in Britain and welfare in much poorer economies.

The way in which these problems were solved was on the whole seen in the Carnegie histories as a very positive acquisition of skill and confidence by government administrators. It was interpreted as a learning process in which the large numbers of businessmen and the other experts hastily recruited into the civil service had a beneficial effect on what had previously been a very small and decidedly conservative group of experts. Wholesale grocers, coalmine owners, shipping magnates, bankers, were given key executive positions and because their habits of thought and action were so different from that of the civil servants the function of **government administration** and its relationship to the economy **was never** likely to be seen in the same passive light again. **On the other** hand it cannot be said that the impact of these **events on the** structure of the civil service and its position in **government was** very great. The Treasury soon brought the **powerful new** ministries and departments under control and **after the war** they mostly disappeared from the scene [13].

That governments learned that they could **do well things** which they had previously regarded as beyond **their competence** is obvious. If the purpose was thought of as **unfortunate,** exceptional and temporary, that mattered less **than the fact** that knowledge and confidence once acquired could **be brought** into play again if needed, as indeed they were **straight away in** the Second World War. The ultimate implications, **spotted by** only a few of the authors of the Carnegie volumes, **were more** complicated. They did not concern the debate, **conducted with** so much vigour, as to whether controls over **the peacetime** economy were or were not more effective than **absence of** government intervention. Rather they concerned **those areas** where the extension of successful government **controls came up** against the boundaries of a wider world where **government** control could not so effectively operate. It is to **these international** considerations that this essay will turn **at the end.** Suffice it to say here that in this wider context **government** intervention and control had necessarily to be **more fumbling** and doubtful. No matter how dominant Britain's **role in the** pre-war international economy there was no **real possibility** that Britain would be able to bend the economy **of the world to** suit British purposes. The resolute, pragmatic **solving of** problems by government intervention in the economy **was very** successful in the narrower national context in **which it was** implemented, but it could not by itself solve the **fundamental** strategic and economic problems of a small island **so heavily** dependent on foreign trade. German strategy **concentrated on** exactly this weakness by launching a large **submarine fleet** against British shipping and supply.

This was a problem whose implications escaped **Bowley and** although it was not ignored by Lloyd, like others **who shared** his wartime experience he nevertheless felt that the successful operation of controls pointed the way towards a less wasteful, a more efficient, capitalism, if only that way could be found.

Lloyd's attitude might be characterised as one of regret that the experiments in economic administration undertaken during the war had been abandoned after 1918 and also as one of certainty that, despite their abandonment, they represented a long-term trend in the modification of liberal capitalism in Britain and thus that their abandonment would prove only temporary. The principal effect of the First World War was therefore, he argued, to accelerate a transformation in the economic system. 'Thirdly', he wrote, 'I am disinclined to admit that *all* the measures of industrial and commercial organisation adopted during the war, which are commonly lumped together under the term state control, were merely necessary evils to be got rid of as soon as possible and never to be thought about again. A considerable extension of co-operative and collective enterprise seems to me probable and desirable in times of peace; and I believe that there is something to be learnt from the experiments in state control during the war which may be of positive value in the difficult times ahead. . . . When the time comes for computing the total net cost of the war and its after-effects, what little there is to be set down on the credit side will need to be sifted with microscopic care from the evil consequences which leap at once to the eye; and among these changes and developments that may appear to some to contain the germs of a better order of society a place may perhaps be found for some features, at any rate, of the experiments described in this volume' [42: *preface*].

Lloyd did not think that the First World War foreshadowed any fundamental change in the economic system, but that it foreshadowed the growth of larger firms organised in associations and trusts, of larger trade unions negotiating at a national rather than a local level, and of the development of state control as a regulating force in the economy, of the elimination of the wastes which he attributed to the more intensely competitive system which had prevailed before 1914. The greater concentration of firms and the greater size of trade unions have been the results of so many converging trends in the twentieth-century economy that it is hardly possible to measure the part played by the war in these processes, but the interest of his book and its subsequent influence depended not only on his excellent account of the development of state interference in the economy but also on the extent to which his forecasts appeared to have been fulfilled in the 1930s. He himself gloomily reflected that all that was left of the war economy were protectionist and nationalist tariffs 'and the economic clauses of a Treaty which threatened to destroy the possibility of stable reconstruction' [42: *371*]. But certain measures of control abandoned between 1918 and 1920 did indeed reappear in various disguises in the 1930s, agricultural price supports and certain tariff devices for example, and those that had not done so by 1939 were quickly reimposed when the Second World War broke out. Organised competition, Lloyd argued, pitted like with like and measured their comparative efficiency with precision; the free play of the competitive system conferred its rewards and punishments indiscriminately. He would certainly have acknowledged the type of capitalism which developed in Britain after the Second World War as being the result, in part, of the First World War.

The rapid abandonment of state controls after 1918 was equally disappointing to those historians who believed that the pressure for social change built up by the war amounted to more than a mere desire to modify the type of capitalism in Britain. R. H. Tawney argued that the dismantling of economic controls was both inevitable and mistaken in so far as it was against the long-term historical trend. His summary of the effects of the war is almost exactly like that of Lloyd. 'The period of war economy accelerated the demise of the individualist, competitive phase of British capitalism. It stimulated organisation and combination among manufacturers; advertised rationalisation; strengthened the demand for tariffs; and encouraged, in another sphere, the settlement of wages and working conditions by national rather than by local agreements' [64; *69*]. Tawney expressed his views cautiously, perhaps conscious that he was a specialist in another period, but more likely impressed by the speed with which the country had returned to 'normal'. There had been, he ruefully admitted, no 'intellectual conversion' to economic control.

But the gross failure of the return to 'normality' in the 1920s, the growth of collectivisation in the 1930s and the success of the economic controls applied in the Second World War cheered those of Tawney's outlook; it may be no coincidence that Tawney should have published his article in 1943. The Second World War was so much more 'total' even than the First that it reawakened interest in the work not only of Lloyd but also of Bowley. Under the pressure of war the same social changes that Bowley had identified earlier took place again and seemed, as before, related to the greater involvement of the population as a whole in the war. This observation provided a further conceptual framework to explain these changes in the functioning of the capitalist economy.

In 1954 Andrzejewski published his theory of the 'military participation ratio' [3]. This was derived from the general idea, frequently discussed after 1914, and implied in Bowley's work, that there was some inherent connection between the extent to which war involved the total population and the extent of social change. Andrzejewski argued that the extent of social welfare in any society varied with the extensiveness of the social groups required to fight in its wars. There is always a gap between the actual military participation ratio, the proportion of those who take part in the fighting to those who are not involved, and the optimum military participation ratio, the ratio that would allow a society to fight its wars most effectively. The relevance of such a theory to the twentieth century is easy to see. Adam Smith had believed that the maximum possible ratio of combatants to civilians was one in a hundred.[7] In both World Wars in Britain the ratio was nearer to one in five. By measuring the gap between the actual and the optimum ratios Andrzejewski argued it would be possible to show which social groups would become involved in future fighting and, more importantly, which social groups would therefore benefit by being able to make their claims on the state felt and thus alter the way in which it functioned.

Titmuss, more cautiously, proposed roughly similar conclusions which he held to have been demonstrated by the changes in social policy during the Second World War [65; 66]. Less crude than Andrzejewski's theory, Titmuss's views are

24

nevertheless closely related. 'Total war' is war of a total society. Previously social policy had been concerned with alleviating the lot of particular groups or classes, the unemployed, the widowed, the old, the orphaned and so on. Only some were involved in unemployment or widowhood; all were involved in war. The bomber did not discriminate. Against its menace the only remedy at first seemed to be to minimise the general panic which would ensue. In March 1939 the Ministry of Health had asked the India Office for the loan of an official used to dealing with large crowds, of the kind that might pour in panic from bombed London. By summer 1940, however, practical relief on the spot was provided for all. School meals were no longer provided only for the 'necessitous', issues of special welfare foods and vitamins were made to all. Old-age pensions were generally increased even in war. The hated household means test for social service payments was abolished. From 1942 onwards, in spite of the war, the general health of British society began to improve strikingly.[8] The implication of Titmuss's views is that the Welfare State as it came to exist in the late 1940s owed its existence by that date to the Second World War. It should not be forgotten that when, during the war, Beveridge issued his more or less freelance report proposing a comprehensive social insurance system which would be obligatory for all citizens it became, for all its arid nature, a bestseller.[9] And the administrative foundations of the future National Health Service were greatly strengthened by the need to organise a national hospital system for civilians during the war.

Andrzejewski's theory has proved too precise for most others to swallow, and historians who are sympathetic to its general implications have found much evidence to tell against it. The aspirations of those caught up in the process of economic and social change generated by both World Wars were vague, formulated within the conventional bounds of the existing political system, and sometimes anachronistic [1; 46; 47; 48]. The Ministry of Reconstruction issued a wide-ranging series of slight reports in 1918 and 1919 outlining and advocating reforms in almost every aspect of administration and policy, but achieved nothing except its own disappearance in the first

25

post-war depression [36]. The 'homes fit for heroes' movement initiated by Lloyd George evoked a peasant smallholding world which in Britain had disappeared for ever. Abrams suggests that the only group which appears to have benefited in terms of Andrzejewski's hypothesis was that of middle-aged propertied women, to whom the franchise was extended [1]. After the Second World War, however, the political change was more marked and in its reconstruction policies the Labour government responded over a longer period of time and with more effort to aspirations for change which had developed in the war. Full employment became a prime political objective, although that is not the reason why it was achieved. Enormous resources at a time of great competition for them were poured into working-class housing. The creation of a much more comprehensive and generous system of social security and health care likewise reflected the apparent popularity of such reconstruction programmes during the war.

In short, the 'military participation ratio' theory is much too crude to explain a complex process of political, social and economic interaction stimulated by large-scale war and the return to peace. Marwick has suggested a more complex matrix in which this interaction might be measured [47; 17]. This matrix would embrace four measurements. It would include firstly the disruptive effects of the war, secondly the testing effects of the war which determine whether any society is capable of adaptation to the new challenges, thirdly the tendency of war to increase participation in the way Andrzejewski suggested, and fourthly the psychological effects, the last being extremely important because, Marwick argues, total war is a 'psychological experience comparable with the great revolutions in history' [17: 4]. Measured in this way the world wars would appear as discontinuities in an historical pattern of gradual economic and social change, greatly accelerating changes under way and abruptly producing new ones also. Many of these changes have been usually considered wholly desirable.

Present interpretations of the impact of the wars on Britain have thus left Hirst a long way behind. His economic analysis is universally seen as far too narrow to comprehend the phenomenon which he was seeking to describe and analyse. Indeed, the two wars themselves are usually held by historians to have been a major cause of the decay of liberal politics and of liberal economic thought. What has replaced Hirst and his numerous like-minded fellows has been an increasingly complex attempt to link the processes of social, technological and organisational change in twentieth-century economies to the economic changes generated by the wars. How far is this justified by our economic knowledge of the wars and how far does it explain the pattern of British history in this century?

In the following section it is argued that the speed and degree of social and organisational change in Britain caused by the wars has been much exaggerated, especially when compared to the economic changes generated by the wars. These economic changes, however, had their impact not so much on the domestic aspects of the British economy as on its international aspects. In that sense the major consequences of the wars for British economy and society have been and are mostly overlooked by the changes of interpretation and in the mode of analysis which have just been described. This does not mean that these changes have not had their own value, or that they are not significant improvements on the liberal analysis as it prevailed before 1914. But to comprehend fully the effect of the world wars on Britain a more comprehensive and less parochial approach is needed and one better founded in the study of *international* economic change. This further problem is considered in the last section.

The Domestic Impact

WERE we to ask a citizen of Germany, the Soviet Union or Japan if he perceived much change in our society over the period from 1914, and were he to use his own society as a yardstick, he would surely reply that he did not. The actual social changes which Titmuss can unequivocally attribute to the wars are neither very numerous nor very impressive: the

27

free treatment of venereal disease, free immunisation against diphtheria, an increase in the number of children provided with milk and meals at school, part of which provision has since been withdrawn, and the abolition of the household means test for social security provision, a test which has in any case tended to creep back in various disguises. On the other hand it is clear that, in a more general way, the Second World War did have an important influence on the transformation of the social security system into something much more comprehensive which took a much higher share of government expenditure.

Beveridge, in most respects as firm a representative of the school of *laissez-faire* liberal thought as Hirst, when asked in the Second World War to produce a report on the social services, took the same pragmatic view as he had of food control and rationing in the First World War and advocated policies of state intervention and help in the normal life cycle of the individual, something which had also become the programme of British socialists. Indeed, in some directions, as in state provision for the aged, his proposals went further than those which the Labour Party subsequently enacted. Like many he had become convinced that the future of liberal democratic society actually required the abandonment of the strict actuarial application of insurance schemes to large sections of the population if they were fully to participate in it. Indeed he enunciated what has since been one of the few identifiable ideological standpoints of the British Labour Party by implying that the comprehensive state provision which he advocated, the Welfare State as it came to be called, would demand the application of the same equal fiscal rules to all members of society no matter what the advantages which they might otherwise be able to buy for themselves. Similarly, the wartime changes in hospital and other medical provision, which Titmuss describes, clearly did make possible the provision after the war of universal, cheap, equal medical provision through medical insurance to which all were forced to contribute whatever their income or position. Yet, at the moment of writing, these new principles of welfare, celebrated at the time as a permanent social and economic reform in consonance with long-term trends, have not only been constantly eroded but are now on the point of being decisively rejected. It is a cautionary note against stressing too strongly the pressures towards such reforms during and after the Second World War to remind ourselves that Beveridge, who had by 1945 become, and has remained, a popular symbol of the Welfare State, was excluded from government influence, pushed out of his Oxford college, and when he stood for parliament defeated in a left-wing landslide not by the left but by a right-wing conservative. To read works like those of Titmuss now is to be aware how much his explanations of apparently irreversible social change are called into question by the fact that the changes have not proved irreversible at all. Likewise, works written in the 1920s demonstrating the way in which war had changed the position of women in society must have rung hollowly in the heads of those many women who were driven out of employment in 1921 never to find a job again.

If we ask ourselves which social changes produced by the wars have proved long-term the most obvious is one not discussed at all by most commentators. It is the dramatic change in fortune which the world wars brought to the agricultural sector of the economy. The effects of the German submarine blockade in the First World War were to lead the British Government in 1917, by the use of financial incentives and by compulsory powers which were hardly used, to attempt to reverse the trend of agricultural development in Britain over the previous forty years. That trend had been a rapid reduction of the importance of agriculture, a rapid shrinking of the labour force, an increase in grassland and in the production of some meats and of dairy foods, and a drastic decrease in many arable crops, particularly cereals. The attempt to reconvert to arable farming in order to combat the German strategy of cutting-off food supply was relatively successful and the crop area in 1918 was greater by 3 million acres than in 1916. The various financial incentives were embodied in the Corn Production Act, 1917, which fixed minimum prices for wheat and oats. The Ministry of Reconstruction advocated the retention of these measures on the statute book in peacetime and the Agriculture Act, 1920, established a system of annual price reviews for farm produce which would maintain the wartime structure of output. Less than one year later, with the onset of the depression, this Act was repealed and the previous trend of agricultural development reasserted itself.

Before the Second World War the government's assumption was that it would be able to manage the economy while still retaining agricultural prices at their pre-war level. There were two reasons why this proved impossible: the increase in imported fodder prices and the powerful and successful pressure which farmers were able to bring to bear on the government in the new circumstances, pressure to which the government rapidly yielded.[10] The occasion of its capitulation was the decision in June 1940 to lay down a minimum national wage for agricultural workers instead of minimum local wages, itself a reflection of the suddenly increased importance of agriculture. Faced with this additional increase in costs, which would have meant an extra annual wage bill for the industry of £15 million, farmers demanded a wide range of higher and guaranteed prices. The effect of their pressure, which was continued throughout the war, appears in an interesting book by Seers [60]. Dividing the income-receivers into various groups and comparing the value of the *per capita* pre-tax income received by each group, he is able to demonstrate that the increase in farmers' incomes between 1938 and 1949 on an average was seven-and-a-half-fold. Certain professional groups alone did better, but when allowance is made for taxation the improvement accruing to them was easily outdistanced by that accruing to farmers. By comparison the improvement accruing to wage-earners on an average *per capita* pre-tax basis was two-and-a-half-fold. Agricultural labourers, of course, did much less well than farmers.

There can be no doubt that not only did the farming community enormously improve its position in the economy as a result of the Second World War, but that that improvement has been a long-term one. The system of guaranteed prices and annual price reviews, acting, as it were, as an insurance taken out by the state on behalf of the farmer against the risk of crop failure, has been maintained in full vigour since 1940. Since the adherence of the United Kingdom to the European Economic Community the guaranteed prices have been internationalised and the mechanisms of protection adapted to conform to those of the Community's Common Agricultural Policy, one of the rare examples where the workings of the capitalist economy have been managed by international agreement. As in the rest of western Europe, in the immediate aftermath of the Second World War agricultural protection on a massive scale became an inherent, almost an unquestioned, aspect of British politics and society. It should be noted, however, that in this transition the influence of the pattern of international trade and payments left behind by the war was also very strong. When only the United States had food surpluses, maximising the amount of food produced in Britain, at whatever cost, could be represented as saving dollars at a time when they were the scarcest currency, and thus helping to resolve the international payments problem. This had not been the case in 1920–1 when the Agriculture Act, embodying many of the same principles, was abandoned.

If we turn to other social groups apparently in a position to benefit, the outcome is less obvious, partly because such groups were more amorphous and often more divided amongst themselves than farmers. Bowley originally identified wage-earners as a group who benefited from the First World War, and subsequent writers suggested that to them should be added those who lent money to the government. The two groups cannot be separated, for the consequences for both were generated by the highly inflationary method by which the government chose to finance the First World War. Inflation is a most powerful cause of social change, and in a period when what was produced by the economy and the rewards distributed for producing it were subject in themselves to drastic change, inflation could only increase the sense of a changing order.

The causes of the inflation in the First World War have received sufficient attention to merit a further book. Simplifying drastically, it could be said that the impact of the war on the international economy was inflationary and that this was exacerbated by domestic financial policy. The demand from all the powers involved for raw materials and finished products was so great as to cause a general rise in the price of imports

31

which in turn caused British wholesale prices to move upwards sharply in the spring of 1915. International demand was sustained on this level throughout the war, but its impact on Britain afterwards was probably less important than the government's own constantly increasing demands on the domestic economy. The government was able to satisfy this demand by borrowing on a massive scale, until 1917 in the form of three separate long-term loans and after that date more by short- and medium-term borrowing. All the forms of paper which the government issued to finance the gap between expenditure and revenue from taxation were in themselves sources of credit. The deficit thus provided for a general increase in purchasing power, the effects of which the government struggled to modify through fiscal policy and controls on the supply of goods. These efforts were noticeably unsuccessful in the first two and a half years of the war and the spectacle of luxury spending by a small number of the especially favoured sharpened the edge of social and economic criticism. To ensure an adequate supply of funds to the government, moreover, the interest rate on money had to be increased repeatedly, only falling after 1917 when economic controls became really effective. Those who lent to the government were therefore able to protect themselves against inflation, while at the same time the government provided them with important concessions in the payment of death duties and, after the war, when reducing the burden of debt, offered them relatively favourable terms of conversion [39; 52].

Hirst, while lamenting the increase in government debt, believed that this process had had one obviously beneficial effect, a wider distribution of capital [33]. Not only were people who had not been accustomed to invest attracted into the investment market by the flood of government paper on favourable terms, but many workers, particularly those in munitions factories, were able to accumulate a considerable fund of savings for the first time in their lives. There was of course a distinct probability that this would be the result of an economy where production for civilian purposes was increasingly restricted and where foodstuffs were rationed and controlled while earnings rose. The idea that such an opportunity

32

should be in fact exploited lay behind Keynes's now celebrated articles, *How to Pay for the War*, which appeared in *The Times* in 1940 [38]. There he pressed for a system of compulsory savings, whereby the increased incomes accruing in the course of the war would be temporarily withheld until after the war. The result would be that the government would be able to borrow more easily during the war and without such apparent social injustice, and after the war, by releasing the extra income, would be able to combat the post-war depression by increasing purchasing power. The working classes would thus be made to liquidate their claims on goods when goods were available instead of liquidating them during the war to the embarrassment of the government. The payment would be made from the results of a capital levy. Wage-earners would be made to reduce some of the inequalities of the capitalist system instead of merely indulging in pleasure.

His ideas were only in part accepted by the government, and in that part wherein they were anti-inflationary [59]. Fear of another inflation of the same kind as in the First World War was the mainspring of Treasury policy. The abandonment of the gold exchange standard in the 1930s and the acceptance of exchange controls, making the impact of international monetary movements on Britain much less direct, together with an immediate strict imposition of physical controls, enabled the government to maintain the interest rate on government long-term borrowing at 3 per cent throughout the Second World War. The whole-hearted acceptance that it was necessary to impose a battery of restrictions and physical controls on the civilian economy and to increase taxation from the outset did mean that the more glaring social inequalities of the First World War were avoided. But the same demand for labour and the same increase in money wages existed even if the incidence of fiscal and financial policy was different; the underlying pressure towards social change was still there.

There is some evidence that Hirst was correct in his supposition that capital became more widely distributed. The War Savings Certificates issued in 1916 were originally intended to be issued only to those who had satisfied a means test, but the government abandoned that test as unnecessary.

The number of small savers did increase, as witnessed by the continuation and success of the National Savings Movement after the Second World War. But these facts have to be seen in proportion. The War Wealth Committee calculated that 68 per cent of the total increase in wealth during the First World War went to that class which already possessed fortunes of more than £5,000, thus suggesting that the previous inequalities may have been intensified. There is a more careful check on these calculations in the work of E. V. Morgan [52]. Before 1914 government securities in private hands were about $2\frac{1}{2}$ per cent of total private property; in the 1920s they had risen to almost 25 per cent. The main owners of all this government paper, however, were extra-budgetary funds and private investment companies, such as the National Health Insurance Fund, insurance companies, banks and firms in the money market. Between 1914 and 1919 small savers absorbed about £487 million of the National Debt, and between then and 1924 a further £131 million. The total debt was £6,592 million. In the tax year 1924–5, £67,923,000 of securities changed hands on the death of their owners; only £1,385,000 were in estates to the value of less than £100. Nevertheless it should also be said that the proportion of securities to the total size of estate was greater in the smaller estates.

Rough measurements of the holdings of capital show that there has been a tendency to redistribution in this century but that that tendency has been very slight. The percentage of the national stock of capital owned by those owning between £1,000 and £5,000 was just under 16 per cent in the period 1911–13; in the period 1924–30 it was about $17\frac{1}{2}$ per cent. There was little change between that date and 1936–8, but between 1946 and 1947 the percentage was about $21\frac{1}{2}$ per cent. That proportion of the national stock held by those holding less than £1,000 increased only very slightly, but the proportion held by those holding over £100,000 fell most markedly [40]. There is thus considerable evidence in favour of a redistribution of capital accelerated by the world wars, but little evidence that this touched the poorest groups. Looking outside the boundaries of Britain again, it is impossible not to be more impressed by the stability of the pattern of capital holding in Britain when compared, for example, to Germany, where capital holdings have twice been almost wiped out, than by these changes. Little is known of the level of working-class savings in the First World War, but studies at the close of the Second World War suggest that there were great inequalities according to the level of income. The poorer 52 per cent of a sample of working-class families studied by Durant and Goldmann in 1944–5 owned only 9 per cent of the aggregate savings total of the sample, while at the other end of the scale 12 per cent of the families owned 50 per cent of the total savings [19]. In general the remarkable thing about the level of working-class savings is how low it was.

So low was the level of soldiers' pay that it is reasonable to suppose that if the wars did provide a boost to the working-class standard of living and thus help to establish a trend towards greater social equality, the rewards must have been distributed arbitrarily according to the occupation of males or the possibility of females taking advantage of the high demand for labour. In certain mass-production processes there came a startling increase in the employment of women. The chief government munitions factory, Woolwich Arsenal, employed only 100 women in November 1916 but 30,000 a year later. At some stages 400 new women a day were being taken on [13]. But the total increase in female employment, about 1,600,000, during the First World War was much less than the increase in male employment in the armed forces. In both wars the increase in civilian employment came also from the unemployed and males at both ends of the age-scale who had previously been excluded and were too young or too old to be taken into the armed forces.[11] It has to be remembered that there were more than a million people registered as unemployed in Britain in April 1940. Nonetheless in the Second World War as in the First the expansion of the armed forces to more than four and a half million meant dramatic changes in labour markets and in the nature of employment. In the Second World War the main instrument of control and planning was the 'manpower budget' which allocated labour resources to the different tasks. The question we have to resolve is how far these bewilderingly rapid shifts of employment had any long-term effect on the economy.

As far as the employment of women is concerned the long-term effects were not very noticeable. Between 1911 and 1921 the total number of females in gainful employment increased by only 234,000. There was a decrease of almost 200,000 in the clothing trade and an increase in metal industries, engineering and shipbuilding. Together with the increase in the civil service, 69,000, this does indicate a certain willingness to accept women in occupations where they had been unwelcome before. But the gains were extremely small. There was very little diminution of the male prejudices which dominated shop- and factory-floor [10] and no serious attempt at all to invest in making it easier for women to work. What is more, after 1921 female employment again declined. The persistence of full employment after the Second World War meant that women did not again fall out of employment to the same extent. The level of female employment in the 1950s was noticeably higher than an extrapolation of the trend before 1939 would imply. Taking a category of employment where the census classifications did not change too drastically, that of transport and communications, the number of women employed was, in 1901, 27,000, in 1911, 38,000, in 1921 between 72,000 and 75,000 depending on the classification used, in 1931, 82,000, and in 1951, 149,000. After 1921 a special classification to indicate clerks and typists was introduced, although it was not always observed in the same manner. The number of women employed in public administration and in commercial occupations increased from 105,000 in 1911 to 668,000 in 1921 by the old classification. Using the new classification and combining the categories of public administration, commercial, financial and insurance occupations, and clerks and typists in order to smooth out certain vagaries of allocation, the number of women so employed was 1,149,000 in 1921, 1,152,000 in 1931 and 2,286,000 in 1951.

In both wars hours of work were long. Yet it cannot be simply assumed that the impact of the demand for labour was to put up the real wages and the standard of living of the largest section of the community. The extent of rationing and other economic controls, together with increasing taxation and rising prices, makes the actual level of real wages and the wider issue of the standard of living difficult to determine. In addition, as several interesting studies have shown, demand for labour was very complex in its incidence.

The level of real wages in both wars has usually been measured by the retail prices collected by employment exchanges from 1914 onwards, which later became the Board of Trade cost-of-living index. On this basis it appears that only in the last year of the First World War was there a *general* substantial gain in real wage rates as opposed to money wages, although it must be remembered that because of overtime pay earnings were often much higher than before 1914. Bowley distinguished sharply between the fortunes of the unskilled workers and those of the skilled artisans. Statistical investigations in five English towns made in 1912–14 and 1923–4 revealed that whereas in 1913 a considerable number of workers, although in full-time employment, did not earn a sufficient wage to keep them out of poverty, this had become very rare by 1924 [7]. Bowley attributed this mainly to the demand for labour during the war forcing up the wage rates of the lowest paid. 'The skilled artisan', he wrote, 'had gained little by 1924, except the reduction of working hours' [8: *160*].

This observation could be taken further; the technological changes in production processes during the war went a long way towards ending the distinction between 'artisan' and 'workman', and what the First World War did not complete the Second World War did. War's high demand for large quantities of standardised articles led to a great increase in the use of single-purpose machine-tools and other mass-production techniques. Nearly a quarter of a million .303-inch machine-guns were manufactured in the First World War, all more or less to a pattern; 849,923 were made in the Second World War. Almost four million rifles were turned out in the First World War [34: *10*]. The tank, not really used in battle until 1917, had by 1918 become a mass-produced good. The aeroplane, still an object of curiosity in 1914, had also entered into the stage of mass production by 1917. The size of the British aircraft industry in 1918 is often forgotten. There were 52,027 military aeroplanes manufactured in the First World War, not much less than half the total manufactured between 1939 and 1944, although of course the earlier machines were simpler. The massive scale of government orders and the urgency to fulfil them led at the start of the war to a great increase in the installation of machine-tools, particularly turret lathes, capstan lathes and universal milling machines, many of which had to be imported from the United States where the general level of mechanisation within the factory was much higher. As the level of orders grew, and as semi-skilled men who operated such machines were taken into the armed forces, the tendency to instal automatic machine-tools which could be used by entirely unskilled labour developed. At the same time older machines were adapted to use by unskilled labour. Not only was there a great increase in the use of machine-tools but also a great improvement in their deployment, especially after the government census of machine-tools in 1915. The gun, aeroplane and tank factories of 1918, in their equipment, layout, employment structure, and methods of organisation, bore little resemblance to most British factories of 1913.

This increase in mechanisation produced similar effects in both wars. At the start, because of the sudden shift of output towards engineering and capital goods, there was a sharp increase in the demand for skilled labour.[12] The high cost of skilled labour then produced a wave of investment, aided by the government, in more capital-intensive methods of production, for which the machinery had in large part to be imported from the United States. In the very first stages of the First World War there was also an increase in the number of those employed in unskilled jobs. Meanwhile, women replaced men in clerical work and in retail trade. As mechanisation proceeded, the need for semi-skilled workers to operate the new machines increased more rapidly than the need for skilled workers. It was this that caused the first 'dilution' agreements of 1915, for the job pattern was changed by taking away from the skilled artisan the more mechanical parts of his job and having them performed on the new machines by the semi-skilled. Since most wages were paid by piece-rates, or had similar incentive bonuses attached, the skilled worker's income

38

was reduced relative to that of the semi-skilled worker. After the conclusion of the Shells and Fuses Agreement in March 1915 the manufacturers began to instal large numbers of automatic machines, which had made their first appearance in boot factories and now began to transform shell factories. With their appearance came the final stage of the concept of the mechanised production line, to spread rapidly from shell factories into many other manufactures. These machines needed only unskilled labour and it was with their installation that women first moved into factory jobs in significant numbers. The Dilution Scheme worked out in October 1915 finally consigned the skilled artisan to the tool-room and saw the replacement of semi-skilled workers by unskilled workers and women [14].

This replacement was accompanied by constant improvements in the earnings of the unskilled, whose whole function in the factory had been changed by this rapid mechanisation. They had achieved greater regularity and formality of employment, albeit at drearily monotonous tasks. This increased formality in the employment structure was then ratified by the changes in the social security system, the most important of which had actually been introduced before the First World War, which made it more difficult for employers to employ unskilled labour on a casual day-to-day basis as and when particular tasks needed doing. The bureaucratisation of the employment structure which accident insurance and social insurance meant, together with the greater formalisation of wage bargaining with trade unions, as well as the increase in numbers and strength of the unions representing unskilled workers which high employment levels produced, all combined to effect an important break in the pattern of employment and existence of the pre-1914 world. The impact of the war on female employment was essentially only a part of this process, not a special phenomenon. By 1917 women were undertaking jobs in many industries which in a different form had been carried out by semi-skilled and even skilled male workers before the war. Indeed the category of 'semi-skilled' lost its former meaning as the need for training diminished and became merely an arbitrary classification for wage-setting.

39

Women simply became part, a small part, of the new industrial proletariat. It is perhaps fortunate that the position and income of all who made up this proletariat had been favourably affected in the long term by the war.

With the particular talents of the semi-skilled worker made superfluous on the factory floor, with the skilled artisans greatly reduced in numbers and influence, with the ability of the unskilled to command for five and a half years higher earnings in regular employment, and with their much greater safety and regularity of employment (if they had a job) in the inter-war period, the gap in economic and social status between these groups narrowed. Many of the fiercest labour disputes of the First World War and not a few in the Second were caused by these important social changes.

Concluding his chapter on changes in income distribution, Bowley drew attention to three trends in particular: the tendency to eliminate 'remediable poverty'; the tendency to diminish 'excessive wealth'; and the tendency to a more equal distribution of incomes. 'The changes are due to many factors, some of which are directly traceable to the war, while others, such as the fall of the birth-rate and the extension of social services, are the continuation of processes that began before the war, which, however, cannot have been without influence on the manner and date of their development' [8: *165*]. These were wise words, borne out by all subsequent research. Winter [70] has subsequently argued that the demographic evidence tends to confirm the view that the First World War marked a watershed in the elimination of 'remediable poverty', especially of the chief cause of such poverty observed in pre-war social surveys.[13]

The evidence for this rests mainly on the great improvement in infant mortality rates in the industrial conurbations. A similar, but less drastic, improvement in infant mortality rates was observed between 1943 and 1945. In the First World War this decline occurred when there was actually less medical provision than before the war and may therefore be attributed to the improved standard of living engendered by higher earnings and more regular employment and to the improvement in social provision. Part of this improvement in social provision arose from the social reforms of the Liberal government introduced immediately before the outbreak of war, such as national health insurance, old-age pensions and the payment of maternity benefit. Another part, however, was directly attributable to wartime intervention. This included family allowances to serving men, free school meals for older children, free milk and food for nursing mothers and infants, rent control, and food rationing.

Could the war alone have had so dramatic an effect on the labour market as to change radically a pattern of employment and existence so long established in Britain?[14] What weight should we ascribe to other forces in this process? If the war were the driving force in such a change it could reasonably be held to have changed the impact of the capitalist economy in a decisive way on as much as a third of the population. Unfortunately the spirit of accurate enquiry into the economic basis of all parts of society which originated in the late eighteenth century has, for most of the period after the Second World War, been replaced by an obsession with 'images' of society. These are much easier for the historian to conjure up and provide a welcome opportunity for fashionable self-indulgence since they usually show a more revealing image of the historian than of society itself. It is astonishing that, in the midst of the current political debate about whether the changes in the social security system attributed to the wars should be maintained, hardly any historians have been interested or determined enough to find out what differences these changes have *continued* to make.[15]

Something may be said of the effect of the Second World War on wage-earners from the studies of Seers [60]. That part of the National Income embraced in the category of wages, forces' pay and social income increased by some £900 million at 1947 prices between 1938 and 1947. The gain was mainly attributable to the redistribution of income, especially away from salary-earners and from net property income. Working-class income in 1947 was 59 per cent of private income, whereas in 1938 it was 55 per cent. The total real net income of the category that Seers identified as working class rose by over 9 per cent, and of that category which he identified as middle class it fell by more than 7 per cent.

If, however, these calculations are made on a pre-tax rather than a post-tax basis, the gain appears as relatively insignificant. It then appears that the greater equality is due more to changes in the taxation system, including the institution of food subsidies, than it appears to have been in the First World War. Taxation had also become more progressive between 1914 and 1918, but to a much smaller degree, such that its most marked effect, rather than to improve the position of those with the lowest earnings, had been to reduce the number of very large incomes. From the figures in the report of the Colwyn Committee it would appear that the principal gainers from this redistribution were those whose incomes were between £200 and £1,000 a year.[16] The incidence of income and supertax combined reduced the highest incomes by one-twelfth in 1914 and by almost one-half in 1925. The number of people with gross incomes above £3,000 in 1913–14 was 32,500, but the number above an equivalent income limit, allowing for the change in prices, by 1924–5 was only 24,000 [8: *138*]. It would appear therefore that the most important force making for an improvement in the working-class position in the Second World War was the increase and greater progressiveness of taxation, and that this was also a powerful influence in the First World War but one whose effects were more limited. This must be attributed in large part to the need to pay for war.

That this improvement was the result of the war more than of the long-run development of the economy appears likely, for it was dependent on certain incidences of fiscal policy. The Inland Revenue criticised Keynes's ideas in 1942, remarking that 'the purpose of the income tax is not the redistribution of income', and in February 1941 Churchill raised violent objections to an increase in income tax on the grounds that taxation of the middle and upper classes could go no further [59: *78*]. The improvement also depended on government policy in respect of foodstuffs and rent. The old-fashioned and inadequate Board of Trade cost-of-living index which measured prices on the level of basic working-class consumption, that is to say on the consumption of those who lived on little more than the minimum standard necessary for existence, was carefully stabilised, when it showed a tendency to rise too rapidly at the start of the war, by the use of food subsidies and rent control. It therefore ceased to measure the true cost of living as it came to have even less resemblance to working-class consumption than it had had before. Higher incomes meant that there was a greater consumption of alcohol, tobacco and amusements, the prices of which, not being included in the index, were not stabilised and therefore were higher [29: *500*; 55]. It is thus very hard to be precise about the movement of real wages during the Second World War. But they do not appear to have played as important a role as price control and taxation. 'The total effect of income tax and price changes up to 1948 was to transfer about £500 million at 1938 prices, some £1,000 million at today's prices [1948], of purchasing power from one-sixth of the United Kingdom to the remainder, cutting the real value of the purchasing power in the hands of the top sixth by some 30 per cent, and increasing the purchasing power in the hands of the remainder by about 25 per cent' [60]. A general fall in real wage rates in 1947 marked the beginning of the end of this process, since carried further by the gradual elimination of food subsidies and rent controls. It is not so much true that a long-run tendency to a redistribution of income in the twentieth century has been very greatly accelerated by the two wars as that a very considerable part of that redistribution, although it may be a long-term effect, may have been limited in its occurrence to the period of the two world wars themselves.

To sum up, there is evidence to support the general arguments of Titmuss, Andrzejewski and Marwick. The particular social reforms purely attributable to the war may be few, but certain groups in society were able to bargain successfully for a much better position. Two such large groups were food producers, because of the danger posed by the restriction of food imports, and unskilled workers, because of the tightening of the labour market. In the second case, combined with technological changes in manufacturing, this was probably a social change of great magnitude. No doubt it would be possible to point to other smaller groups in a similar position, and not only armaments manufacturers. A few further remarks about this process may help to put it in perspective.

Sociological research on the impact of disasters on industrialised societies is instructive. Sorokin, whose work was the starting-point for much subsequent research, considered that disaster, of which war might be considered one example, afforded a particularly favourable ground 'for the emergence of radically different social forms' [62: *120*]. This view has since tended to be modified according to the type of society at which the disaster strikes and the magnitude of the disaster. Form and Loomis in particular have drawn attention to the prevalence of a concept of 'return to normalcy' [23; 24]. As long as there is hope for the future, society will hope that that future will resemble the form of the society which is threatened by disaster. The significance of this heightened sense of the need to recover social equilibrium and to go back to 'normalcy' for the events of the 1920s and the return to the gold standard needs little indication here, the economic literature of the time being shot through with such concepts.

It is here that the comparison with Germany, Russia or Japan is especially interesting. In both wars British government put up a relatively distinguished performance. It did prevent disaster and it did maintain the hope that the accepted norms of economic and social existence would be preserved. The parameters within which changes in the functioning of the economy would be allowed to produce social change were not widened as they were, say, in Germany in both world wars and the parameters of acceptable political change much less so. That the general elections of 1919 and 1945 returned to parliament a significantly different group of politicians from pre-war is true. But compare that for one moment with the events in Russia in 1917 or in Germany in the period 1918–20 or even with the political change represented by the first post-war parliament of the German Federal Republic and the circumscribed nature of the changes in Britain is at once clear.

Indeed, a successfully-conducted total war probably means that the political process analysed by Andrzejewski generates a greater level of social and political harmony whose tendency is to reject and chastise economic and political dissidence much more severely. The Local Armaments Committees which sprang up at the beginning of 1915 raised the spectre of workers' control to the extent that employers refused in many

44

places to allow them to function. The attitude of the employers was bolstered by the Munitions of War Act of that year which even went so far as temporarily to impose a pass-book system on munitions workers whereby they were unable to secure future employment without a report from their previous employer. Those imprisoned and deported without trial in the so-called 'revolt of Red Clydeside' no doubt took a rather tangential view of the democratic process in wartime as described by Andrzejewski, Titmuss or Marwick. Wartime propaganda and post-war myth greatly exaggerated the degree of social unity within wartime Britain and in doing so probably also exaggerated the extent to which post-war changes were caused and politically sanctioned by the experience of war. Was 'the Dunkirk spirit' so prevalent in the British economy? Certainly the evidence of growing tax evasion during the Second World War suggests it was not. It was during, not after, the war that higher direct taxation produced the practice on a large scale of rearranging financial affairs so as to pay as little as possible of the tax burden.

That the government should seize the opportunity of war to promote changes which it might consider desirable rather than necessary was an idea which remained unaccepted, as witnessed by the fate of Keynes's recommendations on deferred pay. At the start of the First World War the state rejected the idea of nationalising the armament firms, and the take-over of the railway companies, which foreshadowed their later reorganisation and nationalisation, was based on merely military considerations. The railway rolling stock remained the property of its private owners. In general the boards and associations which developed with the extension of physical controls were essentially compromises with private interests, both sides being driven to compromise by the desperate nature of the situation. Either the methods and functions of private business were grafted on to a government department, or a group of private firms became temporarily a branch of the public service, as in the case of the United Kingdom Oilseed Brokers' Association. The differences in method of operation were mostly to be explained by market factors. Even where the government 'took possession', as in the case of coalmines or flour mills, the phrase

45

did not imply any effective change of ownership. The government accepted financial responsibility for the results of control and enjoyed the use of the plant for its own ends. As in the First World War so in the Second, most controls were resorted to only when unavoidable. Rent control had its origins in a rent strike. In both wars the idea of a capital levy was rejected. In both the British political system and society were held up as vastly superior to those of the enemy powers.

If the success and stability of government provided a framework in which the sociological tendency to seek a pattern of normalcy could assert itself with especial force, it must also be noticed that another tendency may have mitigated against this. It is one which has received remarkably little attention from historians. The very long periods of time over which fathers and husbands were away from the family, the fact that large numbers did not return, the effects of this on children and on marriage, the changes in families when women became the main bread-winner, may also have twice initiated a complex generational pattern of attitudinal and social change. Was this, too, cut short by the desire to return as quickly as possible to the normal framework of family and the established conventions of society? The psychological consequences of military experience, particularly that of combat, seem frequently, as in the recent case of the Vietnam war where they have been studied, to have been the isolation from the 'normal' social framework of those who have undergone such experiences. For many continental countries after the First World War this is cited as a cause of social and political disorder. Former soldiers were prominent in many right-wing revolutionary movements in such countries as well as in the terrorism which they practised. This is an area where for Britain further historical research might well lead us eventually to some clearer and more convincing conclusions.

What sanctioned economic change politically was not its desirability in itself, the sense that the economy functioned in an unjust way and should therefore be adjusted, but the idea of rational efficiency, a quality much needed to win wars. The economic and social changes which lasted were justified and accepted as a more rational deployment of resources. This was the principal argument for the reorganisation of the railways and the electricity supply industry after the First World War and for the nationalisation of industries after the Second. Collective bargaining for wages on a national rather than a local level, the amalgamation of firms, banks and trade unions, payment of income tax at source, full employment policy after 1945, all were justified by this argument. The Beveridge Report itself could be seen as the apotheosis of this argument, a massive attempt at rationalisation of the whole field of social policy, accepted because the irrational inefficiency of what had been developed in so piecemeal a way could no longer be tolerated in a national emergency.

The closer connection between science and industry which the First World War achieved strengthened this movement towards better management of resources, especially as it was itself encouraged by the miscellaneous collection of scholars, writers and reformers who had for long criticised the British economy and British society for their inefficiency. The Haldane Committee appointed in August 1914 first moved the government along the road to the subsidisation of certain industries of particular strategic importance and where it was judged Germany had developed an advantage. Such industries were later singled out for protection in Britain's first breach with free trade, the McKenna tariff. The Privy Council Committee for Scientific and Industrial Research in their report for 1915–16 made no bones about their views on 'the economic problem'. 'There is already a certain number of large firms in this country who, realising the unity of interest between employers and employed, have systematically striven to raise the standard of living among their workers and to give them a direct interest in the firm's success. Some of these efforts have not been philanthropic; and where they have been so in intention they have been proved by experience not to require any such spur. But the small firm finds it as difficult to provide pensions or clubs as to pay for research laboratories or original workers. We believe that some form of combination for both purposes may be found to be essential if the smaller undertakings of this country are to compete effectively with the great trusts and combines of Germany and America.'[17]

The question might even be raised whether this tendency to better management of resources did not have as strong an effect on bringing about the reforms in public health, including the institution of the National Health Service, as the social pressure from below. Describing the fragmentary nature of provision for social services in 1918, the Ministry of Reconstruction committee on these questions wrote, 'It must not be imagined that the anomalies there discussed are but infractions of some academic ideals of logical order, or are to be condemned as merely falling short of abstract canons of constitutional or administrative theory. The truth is that they touch the people very gravely, and that both individually and collectively the nation suffers through the cross-purposes and lack of system which permeate this huge corpus of ill-organised public effort.'[18] Their proposals were to reconstruct local administration in such a way that an approach to a more genuinely national system of medicine could be created. The medical profession was to be turned into an 'organised army'. Although the wars influenced thinking on public health by making it appear a more urgent problem, they urged it in directions in which it had already been guided, and it ought to be wondered whether the National Health Service did not eventually owe as much to the Webbs as to the wars.

If this is true it may be that it is on the frailty and impermanence of these political and administrative changes on which we should dwell. It was the surge of change in economic conditions which altered the balance of political power sufficiently to force the political changes. But those economic conditions, as is their nature, were not durable. The pursuit of full employment, for instance, as a social and economic good in itself has been abandoned. It is in any case not a policy that could be pursued successfully within the confines of the British economy alone. The pursuit of national efficiency as a goal likewise came up against the infinite uncertainties of the multifarious world in which the British economy earned its wealth. It is a truism of history that one of the main consequences of the two great victories won with such immense effort was a reduction in the relative political and economic importance of the United Kingdom in the world compared to other powers, the United States in particular. In this way they reduced the capacity of the British economy to pursue its own goals when these were unacceptable in the rest of the capitalist world. Those very economic and social changes which war promoted in the national economy it likewise made more difficult to achieve or sustain through its effects outside the national economy.

Any attempt to harmonise rigid domestic economic controls with an efficiently functioning international economic system was likely to fail, unless the rules were set by one country alone. At the end of the First World War there was a brief moment when some of those concerned both in Britain and in France hoped to use their military victory to introduce a system of world-wide food and raw material controls even in peacetime in order to solve their own strategic and domestic economic problems. In effect, the problem which was posed, but not solved, a problem which has haunted governments ever since, was that of how to harmonise an apparent change in the functioning of the capitalist economy at home with the fact that elsewhere, on all the outer boundaries where that economy functioned, the same changes had not only not occurred but were not even wanted. When capitalist economies accepted more or less the same rules and objectives as they had before 1914 this problem was one mainly for social reformers, socialists and revolutionaries. As soon as the changes produced by domestic economic intervention were thought of by those who had previously directed these economies as positive and to be retained, a political problem which was to dominate twentieth-century capitalism emerged. A change in the nature and purpose of the capitalist economy at home might be unachievable without a conscious effort to organise the international capitalist economy to at least allow such changes to be maintained. How could the international workings of capitalism be consciously organised in such a way? This problem has been beyond the frail degree of international political agreement in our century except for very brief periods of time. If a way out was to be found it was not in the power of the United Kingdom alone to pursue it. It is therefore to the problems of the British economy in the wider world and the way in which

49

without any accurate assessment of the process of economic development which had made them possible. The hazy minds of politicians were, nevertheless, penetrated by some fear, not of defeat, but that even victory might result in a fatal weakening of the economic basis of British society or, for narrower and more selfish minds, the loss of those privileges and pleasures which that society accorded to them. It was from this mixture of somewhat dimly perceived economic realities and political selfishness that the strategy of 'business as usual' evolved.

It rested on the proposition that the war must involve the minimum amount of disruption to the world-wide network of trade and payments which sustained the British economy and it was true that this did, indeed, as far as possible have to be the basis of any British strategy. But to suppose that there would not, however well conceived the strategy, be a very serious disturbance to the international situation of the British economy was crassly optimistic. And to suppose that Germany might be defeated without a military campaign on the mainland on such a scale as to produce major economic changes in the way the international economy functioned was foolish and escapist. In such a war, no matter how correct the initial strategic premisses, there could be virtually no 'business as usual'. Britain's international advantages had to be exploited and that meant abandoning many of them to maximise the gains from others, a process which was bound to have the most serious repercussions, not on Britain alone but on all the other many countries whose economies were largely involved in the same network of trade and payments.

About half the meat consumed in Britain, more than half the dairy produce, more than two-thirds of the bread grain and flour, about half of the iron ore and all the cotton were imported before 1914. A Royal Commission on the Supply of Food and Raw Materials in Time of War, reporting in 1905, opined that with enough money and enough ships there would be no danger.[19] The cost of these imports was easily met by the earnings from exports together with invisible earnings. The Chancellor of the Exchequer gave his opinion in 1914 that Britain could pay for five years of war from the earnings of its foreign investments alone.

51

But the value of foreign investments in time of war is an uncertain affair. In 1917 some of the massive investments which had built up the infrastructure of the economy of the United States in the nineteenth century were being sold off on the New York stock exchange at values far lower than the book values they had had in the Treasury reckoning in 1914, in order to obtain dollars to purchase essential imports from America. The other major source of invisible earnings, shipping receipts, suffered from the fall in the volume of world trade caused firstly by the disruption of well-established trades and later by the great danger on the high seas, particularly from attacks by German submarines. Germany's strategy increasingly concentrated on attacking Britain's international supply lines. These developments, not hard to foresee, caused a drop in Britain's invisible earnings in the first full year of the war. This would not have been so serious had there not also been a steep fall in visible exports. This was mainly caused by the fact that 'business as usual' had been so little thought out as a strategy, indeed it amounted to little more than a slogan, that it was tacitly abandoned almost from the start. By Christmas 1914 more than a million men had been recruited into a new army to fight on the continent. The production effort needed to supply them led to a fall in exports and, more importantly, to the beginning of a series of interventions in the economy which made international 'business as usual' no more than a dream. In 1915, too, the inadequacy of pre-war planning and the assumptions on which it had been based was also shown up by a severe balance of payments problem with the United States, a steep fall in the value of sterling, and a run on the reserves.

In that year a problem which had become inherent in the British economy from the mid-nineteenth century onwards, but which until the start of the First World War had been easily coped with, presented itself in full force and has seldom been long absent since. How could an economy, so large a proportion of whose national income originated in international transactions, between 25 and 30 per cent, continue to pay for the great excess of imports over exports which it consumed, once the network of international transactions by which this had been managed in 1914 began to break apart under the pressures of war? For Britain the impact of the world wars on patterns of international activity has been often seen by historians as harmful in two different dimensions.

The first has been the generalised impact of the wars on the whole international mechanism of trade and payments. Before 1914 this was still very much a product of the nineteenth-century development of the British economy itself and thus worked in many ways to Britain's advantage, but the international payments mechanisms which have succeeded the pre-1914 'gold standard' have been less flexible, less comprehensive, less durable and have not always operated to the advantage of the United Kingdom. In part this has been because the economic weight of the United Kingdom compared to other economies which influence these mechanisms, particularly to that of the United States, has shrunk. It is this which has given rise to the second area of historical discussion. Were the economic gains which both world wars brought to the United States and the economic difficulties which they brought to Britain such as greatly to accelerate what might otherwise have been a much more gradual change? And did this acceleration fundamentally weaken the British economy by facing it suddenly with a set of international circumstances to which it would otherwise have had a much longer period of time to accommodate itself? To these two issues raised by historians should be added a third, obvious in the context of the previous section. What connections have there been between the domestic economic and social changes so far discussed and the changes in the pattern of international exchanges? It is an interesting irony of the wars that they appear to have accelerated a set of domestic economic and social changes in Britain which have been generally construed as beneficial, while at the same time accelerating a set of international economic changes which may have made these changes in the domestic economy more difficult to support and maintain.

Although the First World War proved a highly inflationary experience the upward movement of prices was not consistent over different categories of goods and values and therefore a precise financial measurement of the changes it brought to Britain's external position is difficult to make. Even rough

53

calculations, however, show how different the reality turned out from the way pre-war strategic thinking had foreseen. In spite of the sharp upward movement of prices the value of domestic exports fell even in current prices in 1915. In real prices it fell to the level of ten years before, wiping out in one year the gains from the great export boom of the last decade before the war. By contrast, re-exports, goods produced elsewhere but brought into Britain solely to be exported again, fell only slightly in value in real terms. The weakness in Britain's trading position lay, firstly, in the high levels of domestic demand generated by the war and especially by the arming and equipping in so short a period of time of land forces of a size not seen for a century and, secondly, in the unregulated struggle for labour and raw materials in which those with military contracts could outbid exporters. The subsequent wartime history of exports was erratic. In 1916 they made a powerful recovery although even in current prices they remained well below the 1913 level. In 1917 they fell again and in that year there was also the start of a precipitous fall in re-exports which continued into 1918, making their level by the end of that year in real terms about a quarter of the 1916 level. Domestic exports also continued to decline in the last year of the war.

The performance of the different export sectors tells us more. In the more important areas of pre-war exports the steepest fall was in machinery and in ships. By contrast, cotton goods, after falling very steeply in 1915, thereafter recovered strongly. There was not in the First World War the almost total sacrifice of staple exports on the altar of war production that the Second World War witnessed. After the nasty shock to Britain's external position in 1915 the economy showed much resilience, demonstrating that the strategic concepts of the pre-war period were not entirely foolish. But the damage done to invisible earnings and exports in 1915 had, as we shall see, important political repercussions. And once we turn to the other side of the external problem, imports, it becomes clear that there the problem was one of much greater magnitude with more far-reaching implications.

The manufacturing base of the British economy proved

inadequate to sustain both the military effort and exports at the same time without additions to the import bill of a wholly unforeseen dimension. The value of imports in real terms increased in every year of the war. In 1914 exports and re-exports fell short by £170.4 million of paying for the total import bill. In 1915 the gap was £367.9 million; in 1918, £783.9 million. Worse, changes in the direction of foreign trade meant that a greater proportion of imports had to come from the United States and thus be paid for in dollars. In 1914 imports from the United States were 18 per cent of British imports; in 1918 they were 39 per cent of the total. The reason was not so much the closure of large areas of Europe to British trade. Firstly, it was the fact that only the United States could supply capital goods and armaments on the scale which the British economy needed to import them. Secondly, as the agricultural sectors of less-developed economies were cut off from the supply of inputs from the developed world on which they depended their output fell, but the less fragile agricultural sector of the American economy produced an increasing share of the world's food surpluses. Britain had already had a large deficit, £82.2 million, on visible trade with the United States before the war, but this had been partly settled through British export surpluses to third markets, particularly India, which in their turn had export surpluses to the United States, and partly by a large volume of British invisible earnings in the United States. The visible trade deficit with the United States in 1918 was £488.6 million.

Yet both the general trade deficit and the specific dollar deficit were only problems in so far as they could no longer be met by receipts from invisible earnings. On the eve of the war, at the end of a period which had seen a remarkable boom in foreign investment, invisible earnings from United States sources amounted to about £1,948 million annually, far more even than the trade deficit of 1918. The total book value of British investments there, built up through the nineteenth century, was between ten and eleven times as much. The quantity of investments sold off to purchase American imports or deposited as securities against loans from the United States and not redeemed was small in comparison to the pre-war quantity. It amounted to about £250 million, so that the overall post-war earning capacity of British foreign investment was not seriously weakened. It was, indeed, far more weakened by the general damage which the war did to the whole of the pre-1914 trade and payments network through which international capital transactions had flowed with such ease. Nevertheless, the fall in dollar earnings combined with the increase in the need for dollars to pay for imports weakened the exchange rate of the pound against the dollar, threatening to make dollar imports relatively more expensive.

This tendency was vigorously reinforced by the exceptional arrangements made between Britain and her allies to pay for the costs of the war, arrangements to which the United States became a party after it joined the war in 1917. Normal accounting and payments settlements were suspended between Britain and France, Britain providing liberal loans to cover the cost of exports to France to sustain the war effort there. France followed the same principle with Russia and, eventually, the United States did the same for Britain, and to a smaller degree, for France, each country allowing massive debts to accumulate with one of its partners on the assumption that in the post-war world the international position of the debtor would soon be strong enough to regulate the situation. Britain lent its allies about £1,419 million and borrowed, mainly from the United States, about £1,285 million. The *overall* financial position of the country therefore justified the pre-war optimism; a nation whose markets were of major importance to so many suppliers and with so much international financial leverage could, indeed, pay its way through the war. But the specific financial relations of Britain and the United States were another matter altogether. Here Britain had very little leverage. The United States became a creditor on a massive scale and saw no reason not to demand the advantages which its position gave it. This stance was upheld after the war as well. When the new Russian government repudiated its war debts the United States continued to demand repayment in full from Britain and France, so that the apparently basically sound overall British balance of payments position proved illusory and the events in Russia left the United Kingdom with far bigger dollar debts than had been foreseen.

The large war debts, made worse by the demands that Germany pay 'reparations' for the loss supposed to have been inflicted on the economies of the Allies, proved a heavy burden on the international payments mechanism when it was painfully reconstructed after the war. The question to be resolved, however, is whether it was the impact of the war on the channels of international trade and payment which was responsible for the relatively poor performance of the British economy in the inter-war period. The war, it was commonly argued, had caused a great expansion in the output of certain industries, coalmining, shipbuilding, steel manufacturing and, above all, in the output of agricultural produce, but in the 1920s demand for such high levels of output was no longer present.[20] Under these strains the international financial system collapsed in the great crash of 1929. The corollary of this theory was that *per capita* incomes were too low and thus produced 'underconsumption'. These arguments seemed to have a peculiar relevance to Britain in the 1920s in view of the fact that unemployment was so heavy in a certain limited number of industries. It should be remarked that these phenomena did not reappear after the Second World War and therefore this argument needs to be examined very closely. The growth in world production over the period 1913–25 appears to have been approximately 1.5 per cent per year, which does not seem excessive. Before these arguments are made to have a special applicability to Britain alone, the meaning of 'overproduction' and 'underconsumption' should be carefully defined. When this is done they will be found to be only relative concepts, dependent for their definition on certain more important aspects of the international economy.

This was the view taken, although rather vaguely, by the Balfour Committee on Industry and Trade which examined the permanent harm done by the loss of markets to British exporters during the First World War.[21] The most serious loss, statistically at any rate, was the decline of 53 per cent in the export of cotton piece goods to India between 1913 and 1923.

Only one-quarter of that decline, however, was attributed by the committee to the development of the Indian cotton-goods industry during the war or to problems of international payments. The total value of British exports to South America fell by over one-third over the same period, allowing for the change in value of the pound, the biggest part of the drop being attributable to the loss of the Argentinian market to the United States, which was much more attributable to the war. The question of the impact of the war on Britain's overseas position was not finally resolved, but the war was not seen as a main cause of the weakening of that position. Of course this does not eliminate the argument that, had it not been for the First World War, British industry would have had more time to adjust to a situation in the 1920s which might have developed more gradually.

After the Second World War the acute difficulties in earning dollars which beset the British economy were also attributed to the effects of the war on the pattern of foreign trade. It was argued that the British economy could no longer earn dollars by its exports to third markets, such as India or Malaya, to pay for its import surpluses from the United States, because the war had not only made the United States a more self-sufficient economy but had altered the geographical pattern of its foreign trade. American imports, it was argued, were a smaller proportion of national income than before 1939 and now came more from the 'dollar zone': Latin America and the Caribbean.[22] In fact, however, these changes in the pattern of American foreign trade were temporary and by 1947 the pre-war pattern was already reasserting itself. The difficulty in earning dollars in foreign trade, part of a world-wide phenomenon, had other causes. It was the result of a remarkable investment boom in the whole of western Europe including Britain, and perhaps elsewhere, which in turn led to a great increase in dollar imports. It is true that this increase would have been less had Germany not been eliminated as a supplier of capital goods on the world market, but not so much less as to eliminate the payments problems which arose for Britain.[23] The investment boom was by no means simply caused by replacing the capital 'lost' in the war and the international payments difficulties which Britain experienced were as much or more a consequence of these domestic decisions as of the impact of the war on international trade and payments.

As for the problem of international payments, it can be readily agreed that the collapse of multilateral trading mechanisms and the subsequent arrival of currency and trade controls on a massive scale from 1931 onwards was in part due to the consequences of the First World War. But did the British economy actually perform worse in the 1930s within a much more fragmentary international payments mechanism and with world trade stagnating than it had after 1925 when multilateral trading mechanisms and currencies freely convertible into each other or gold had been restored according to the pre-1914 pattern? It does not seem so. There was, indeed, a powerful undertow of opposition in Britain after 1945 to the American plans to recreate currency convertibility and a multilateral trading mechanism as the basis of the post-war settlement. This opposition was precisely on the grounds that entry into such a system would prevent the United Kingdom from safeguarding the beneficial social and economic changes which the Second World War was thought to have brought. There would, it was argued, be no protection in such a system for full employment and the Welfare State against the depression which would emanate from the American economy. The multilateral payments system which was agreed on, the so-called Bretton Woods System, was, however, a victim of very early infant mortality. It collapsed straight away in 1947 under the weight of the vigorous investment boom. Bilateral trade and currency controls came back in greater force than in the 1930s. Trade controls were effectively modified after 1952, but only within western Europe, by the trade liberalisation programmes of OEEC and from 1950 onwards the European Payments Union provided a mechanism for multilateral trade within western Europe alone. It was not until 1958 that a world-wide system of currency convertibility similar to that before 1914 or between 1925 and 1931 was restored, and until that time Britain was able to discriminate massively against American trade. It is not possible to see any correlation between the performance of the British economy and these abrupt changes in the international trade and payments system.

By the meanest calculation the boom which began in 1945 lasted for twenty-three years and although there were cyclical troughs, by earlier standards they were insignificant. Of 'overproduction' nothing was heard, although the industries which were expanded in the Second World War were much the same as in the First. The idea of 'underconsumption' would have been an absurdity. It is impossible to accept the suggestion that damage done by the world wars to the international network of trade and payments weakened the international position of the British economy. Indeed, there is some evidence that the economy performed better in more restrictive and less flexible international systems, better in the 1930s than in the 1920s, and better before 1958 than after.

The most dramatic change wrought internationally by the First World War was that in the position of the United States from international debtor to international creditor on a large scale. It was accompanied by a change in the relative manufacturing strengths of Britain and the United States. The United Kingdom's manufacturing base had proved inadequate to sustain a war of mass production on such a scale and its deficiencies had been made up by imports of capital goods, ships and steel from America, with a consequent stimulus to output there. Much the same was true of the relationship between France and the United States. American steel output rose by 15 million tons during the war, about the equivalent of Britain's total output. The output of the American shipbuilding industry by 1919 was half as great again as that of the British. Many of the armaments used by the British forces could only be mass produced by imported American machine-tools. In effect, the war exposed as a weakness a characteristic of British manufacturing industry which had been noticeable in the previous three decades.

The nineteenth century had been so dominated by both the image and the reality of Britain as the world's most powerful industrial nation, 'the workshop of the world', that only sharper insight had perceived that it had remained just that, the world's workshop rather than its factory. The serious

60

labour disputes discussed in the previous section showed how entrenched the position of the artisan had become in the British economy. They reflected important differences in the structure of industry in the major combatant powers. The comparative international advantage of the British economy before 1914 lay precisely in the high level of labour skills on which it could draw and it had been good economics, in the short run at least, to exploit that advantage. In wartime it proved no advantage at all; German and American manufacturing industries at the start of the war were more modern, more capital-intensive, specialised more heavily in capital goods, and proved better suited to cope with the demands of war. The general tendency of export growth in the twentieth century has been for the ratio of exports to output to be higher in those manufacturing sectors where productivity was higher, so that the pressures towards greater capital-intensiveness in wartime manufacturing industry were in accordance with long-term trends in international export growth in peacetime. Britain's international payments difficulties with the United States were not a transient wartime phenomenon caused by a temporary, and reparable, breakdown in the multilateral payments network in which the British economy had functioned. They were but the international symptom of a fundamental shift in the relative domestic economic strengths of the two countries which had already taken place.

What historians have significantly failed to do has been to undertake a coherent long-term analysis of the extent to which the experience of the world wars did force British industry away from the world of the skilled artisan and towards a situation where it was able to find comparative advantages through higher levels of productivity. This failure is the more astonishing because of the acrimony of the present political debate in Britain. All through the general election campaigns of 1979 and 1983 the point was stridently made that it was those social changes, loosely called 'The Welfare State', which have been discussed earlier in this book which had increased costs and lowered the level of productivity in British industry to the point where it was no longer able to compete in international markets, unless some of those changes were undone. Yet, as all

61

historians have observed, the rapid mechanisation of many sectors of manufacturing industry in the First World War was such as to produce a sharp upward movement in productivity. What impact did this have on exports of manufactured goods in the 1920s? Did Britain remain essentially 'the workshop of the world' in the 1920s or was there a significant change in the commodity composition of British exports in that period related to changes in the manufacturing process and to consequent higher levels of productivity, compared to the period before 1914? And what was the effect of trade controls and changes in the geographical distribution of exports after 1931 on this process if it occurred? This last question is of particular importance because, as we shall shortly see, once rearmament began again on a large scale in the 1930s the need for imports of capital goods from the United States again produced a balance of payments crisis with that country similar to that of 1915. Had the manufacturing changes in the First World War not, in fact, by 1938 effected any significant alteration in Britain's position? This pamphlet is short and only about the wars, but from the numerous other books on this question no clear answer emerges because the question does not seem to have been very clearly put.

In the Second World War the tensions over increased mechanisation seem to have been very much less, and occurred as frequently between government and employers as between government and labour. There were some similar examples to the labour problems of the First World War, the displacement of riveters in shipyards for example. But the delay in switching to mass production of vital armaments was much less evident. Indeed, for many items such as shells which had caused problems in 1915, the government had prepared 'shadow factories' in advance, into which unskilled female labour was eventually drafted. Yet the pattern of imports associated with rearmament indicates clearly that these successes still depended on a very large increase in imports of machine-tools and machinery. In that respect the United Kingdom economy had not overcome by 1938 the weaknesses which became apparent in 1915.

The present situation of the United Kingdom is that of a

rapidly declining industrial power whose output and exports are no longer of central importance to the world economy and which is dependent for the defence of its vital interests on American nuclear armaments over which it may itself have no proper control. Its domestic economy, however, is as subject as ever to the influence of the changing patterns of international economic transactions on which the dominant influence is also that of the United States. All this is a stark contrast to the apparent relative position of the two countries in 1913. The stages of this transition and the role which the world wars played in it are now becoming an interesting issue of debate amongst historians. Is it because of the two world wars that the United Kingdom has become in the space of seventy years no more than an occasionally awkward satellite of the United States?

Burk has traced the development of British-American relationships during the First World War and her conclusion is that the American government calculatedly seized on Britain's dollar payments difficulties and, by refusing to maintain the sterling–dollar exchange rate at its existing level in 1917, pursued a policy of replacing London by New York as the world's leading financial centre [12]. That such an opportunity would present itself did not look too probable at the start of the war. Although the outbreak of war provoked a financial crisis it was soon alleviated by the government placing its own credit behind approved commercial bills payable by enemy debtors or by debtors who were unable to meet their liabilities or meet the sudden increase in shipping insurance costs. After that the movement of sterling was towards London until November and the Bank of England's gold reserve increased almost threefold in that time. Before 1914 the Bank of England's gold reserves had never been very large, because a small increase in the interest rate had been enough to bring short-term capital flooding back into London. The differential interest rates offered to attract foreign deposits after August 1914 appeared to be having the same effect. The marked deterioration in the trade balances in 1915 and the rapidly growing volume of imports from the United States, however, began a slide in the value of the pound against the dollar in September of that year.

By 1916 almost all British imports of munitions, iron and steel, oil, cotton and grain were coming from the United States so that by the time the United States entered the war, in Brand's words, 'The British Government, with commitments in the United States running into hundreds of millions of pounds, was at the end of its tether. It had no means whatever of meeting them' [9: ix]. The enormous purchases made in the United States by all countries had transferred a large part of the world's gold reserves to that country. The mechanism by which gold had previously been brought back into London no longer worked and without American support the pound would have to be devalued against the dollar thus putting up the cost of British imports. Although with the American entry into the war the volume of United States lending to Britain was increased to enable the United Kingdom to meet its commitments the United States Treasury still refused to include in its purchases of British Treasury bonds sums intended for the support of the exchange rate. Eventually in March 1919 the pound was officially devalued and taken off the gold standard. Any new multilateral payments system would be at a different pound–dollar relationship. The United States in fact retained all the British securities which had been deposited as collateral against war loans until 1923 when Britain finally, with great reluctance, agreed to the schedule of war debt repayments proposed by Washington.

However, as all studies of the 1920s have shown, Washington's attempted seizure of the dominant role in world financial markets was not very firm. New York banks co-operating in the post-war financial reconstruction of the European economies did so very much in a private capacity and their liaisons with their government even at the time of the Dawes Plan were almost covert. Britain's international financial situation, as measured by the overall balance of payments, had remained relatively sound during the war. If the relative economic strengths of the two countries on international markets continued to alter in America's favour, as they did during the 1920s, this was not because of successful American efforts to exploit Britain's dollar payment problems during and immediately after the war, but because of the different domestic experience of the two economies. It was because productivity levels and growth in the American economy were higher than those in Britain. And although there were important international reasons for lower productivity and growth in the British economy they were not by any means all, or even mainly, to be ascribed to the changes wrought in the international economy by the war. Burk's analysis is essentially of American *policy*; Britain's capacity for economic independence may have been determined more by the complex and swiftly changing economic realities of the post-war world.

The domestic economic recovery in the 1930s was not, compared to that in Germany, in those sectors which were particularly relevant to another war of mass production. After the collapse of the reconstructed international payments system in 1931–3 the British economy did not find in imperial preferences and the Sterling Area a promising alternative to the international benefits of a genuinely multilateral international trade and payments system. As the likelihood of another war with Germany or Japan or both increased there was now less possibility that the necessary dollar imports could be financed by earnings from exports and invisibles. In the absence of a multilateral payments system settlements with the United States had to be made in dollars or gold. Over the period 1934–8 the average annual trade deficit of the United Kingdom with the United States was £62.2 million, while the Sterling Area had a surplus of £15.8 million. The main source of dollar earnings in the Sterling Area, however, was Malaya, India being the only other substantial dollar earner. It was no longer possible to imagine that 'business as usual' would permit the continuance of those distant trades. Total earnings in all currencies from shipping and overseas investment amounted to an annual average over the same period of £345 million. The proportion of this earned in dollars is impossible to determine properly, but investments in the United States and Canada in 1938 were subsequently valued at £4,674 million.[24] The total value of the gold reserves was £836 million in March 1938. If this last sum were to be considered as the ultimate war chest by the Treasury, as it was, the situation was dangerous, for its value was about as high as that of total expenditure on the First

65

World War up to the end of March 1915. On the other hand, as in the First World War, the sale of dollar-earning investments would provide a much greater margin for the purchase of imports, at the expense, of course, of the post-war balance of payments.

Parker argues that American financial policy in 1938 and 1939 compelled the United Kingdom to reduce its gold reserves in order to maintain the pound–dollar exchange rate (unavailingly as it proved) as the trade balance with the United States worsened under the pressure of rearmament. Thus, he argues, even before the war Britain finally lost its capacity for independent action, being forced into subservience either to the United States or to Germany [57].

There are several difficulties with this argument. Before considering them it is important to emphasise that Parker is certainly right in stressing that American policy, as in the First World War, sought to dominate the United Kingdom as an influence on the reconstruction of an international framework for economic activity after the war. All American plans for reconstruction were aimed at the recreation of a multilateral international payments system. This was seen as the guarantee of a democratic capitalist world order which in turn would serve as a guarantee of America's own future economic and political interests. After the events of the 1930s it was feared that the United Kingdom would be a major obstacle to a reconstruction on these principles, that the second successful experience of wartime planning and controls there, combined with Britain's growing international difficulties, would lead the British government to maintain its bilateral trading arrangements, its trade and exchange controls, and its other discriminatory trade arrangements which had been evolved in the 1930s. Given the enormous weight of Britain in international trade this would make American post-war plans impossible to achieve. Accordingly, the United States used all the leverage it could to bend Britain to its will and establish it and the pound sterling as a second pillar of a new post-war multilateral payments system. Between February and May 1940 the British government struggled against American pressures by diverting economic resources to an export drive to build up its reserves.

But this new version of 'business as usual' was abandoned with the German invasion of France. The policy which America had pursued in 1938 and 1939 was continued even after American entry into the war. Continuous pressure was exerted throughout the war never to let British reserves go above $1,000 million (£250 million), so that at the end of the war Britain's bargaining position would be weaker. Similarly, there were more forceful measures than in the First World War to make the United Kingdom strip itself of its American investments, even at low prices, to pay for dollar imports or secure dollar loans. The Mutual Aid Agreement of 1942 which systematised the conditions for mutual military supply in wartime extracted a promise that there would be no post-war discrimination in international trade. By this was meant the imperial preference agreements which made it harder for American exports to penetrate Sterling Area and Canadian markets.

Whether Parker's conclusions are ultimately justified, however, depends on Britain's overall dollar position during and after the war and also on the actual outcome of events after the war. The value of United Kingdom imports from the United States rose from £118 million in 1938 (which in itself was one-third of the level to which the reserves had been reduced at the start of the war) to £532 million in 1944. Exports to the United States fell from £50 million to about £25 million at the same time. Britain's overall deficit on commodity trade increased from £387 million in 1938 to £994 million in 1943, so that the dollar trade deficit was an even larger part of the total trade deficit than in the First World War. This, however, was very much a function of the special financial arrangements which were made even before America's entry into the war. At the end of 1940, the Lend-Lease programme began. Under this programme the United States provided supplies without current payment but against a post-war reckoning, not unlike the arrangements which had prevailed towards the close of the First World War. It was, of course, only this arrangement which permitted so immense a deficit on visible trade with America. The total net book value, after the value of British supplies to the United States have been deducted, of American Lend-Lease supply to Britain was about £5,210 million.

Supplies under Lend-Lease were, nevertheless, at a lower level than imports paid for in cash until the end of 1942. The cash imports were paid for by loans, mainly raised against the value of British investments in the United States and by the sale of British dollar investments. As before 1914, the idea that the volume of supply needed from the United States could be paid for out of the reserves, an idea which was still considered even in spring 1940, looks ludicrous in retrospect. The value of French aircraft orders in America taken over after the collapse of France was £152 million alone, a third of the available reserves! Large sums therefore still had to be raised by borrowing and the sale of dollar investments. The sale of securities is estimated to have brought in about £1,100 million. In addition, before Lend-Lease goods began to arrive there was a loan of about £105 million from the Reconstruction Finance Corporation.

None of these devices would have coped with the overall situation had not the United Kingdom been able to obtain a massive volume of supply from Sterling Area countries against the accumulation of sterling balances by those countries in London. The consequence of this was to transform many of the Sterling Area countries into creditors to Britain on a massive scale. For example, British exports to India dropped from £34 million in 1938 to £18 million in 1943, many British investments in India were sold off to the Indian government, and India accumulated a sterling balance by the end of 1945 of £1,321 million. By the same date and through a similar process Middle Eastern countries, in particular Egypt and the Sudan, accumulated sterling balances of over £500 million. Not only did these transactions substantially reduce Britain's future invisible earnings, but they represented a heavy claim on Britain's real resources after the war. Post-war exports would have to pay for a large part of the imports of the war years as well as those of the post-war period. Yet these transactions themselves show what scope the Sterling Area still gave Britain for manoeuvre independently of the United States. It is true that if these balances were to be paid back at the end of the war this could only be done with American financial help. But they were not paid back and there was an important body of opinion which wished to retain them together with the Sterling Area exchange controls as they had evolved during the war precisely as a defence of the British economy against American post-war reconstruction policies.[25]

One uncertain area in Parker's arguments concerns the actual volume of British dollar investments and how utilisable or saleable they were. The amount of dollars realised by their sale during the war was three times the size of the reserves at the outbreak of war. British income from all foreign investments in terms of gross receipts from interest payments was only about £50 million less in 1946 than before the war. Interest payments of this kind vary of course, according to the profitability of the investment in any one year, itself a function of the state of the economy in which the investment has been made. What is needed to resolve this question is a full study of how much British investment there was in North America in 1938, how much was sold, under what conditions and at what prices. Until that is undertaken the American argument in 1938 that Britain was far from dependent on its reserves to pay for dollar imports remains unrefuted and Parker's arguments unestablished.

A further problem with Parker's arguments is that the post-war multilateral trade and payments system into which the United States was determined to force Britain as the price of wartime aid never in fact came into existence. Its general principles were agreed to by the countries, including Britain, attending the United Nations Conference at Bretton Woods in July 1944. In August 1945 the Lend-Lease agreements were abruptly terminated by the United States without any provision for Britain to pay for those commodities on order or in the course of being delivered. Their value amounted to £161 million. Exports had been reduced to an extremely low level. In 1944 domestic exports were only £266 million, about 60 per cent of their 1938 value, and although in 1945 they recovered very strongly under the pressure of government policy and high demand to £399 million this was hardly enough to cover a total import bill in that year of £1,104 million. In terms of the need to pay for dollar imports the imbalance was greater. Domestically produced exports to the United States in 1945 amounted to

69

£18.6 million; total imports from there amounted to £320.8 million. If Britain were to honour its commitment to the creation of a new multilateral payments system, and the majority of political opinion in the country felt that this would be in Britain's long-run best interests, there appeared no alternative but to seek a further American loan to cover the period until exports and invisible earnings had risen to well above pre-war levels in order to pay off all the international debts which had been accumulated as well as sustaining the high post-war import needs.

The terms of this loan and the terms of settlement of Lend-Lease were agreed together in the Anglo-American Financial Agreements of December 1945. The debt for goods supplied in wartime under Lend-Lease was wiped out. American surplus property in Britain was sold cheaply to the British government. The Lend-Lease goods on order or 'in the pipeline' at the time the Lend-Lease agreements were cancelled had to be paid for in full. In return for this generous financial settlement, which was in vivid contrast to the aftermath of the First World War, the United Kingdom had to agree to make sterling earned on current account freely convertible into dollars under certain safeguards by July 1947. This would ensure that the two currencies would be the centre of the new multilateral payments system into which other countries and currencies would be drawn. To make this system operable Britain would also have to subscribe to the ending of all other forms of trade discrimination. To enable the British economy to go through with this drastic change from the restrictive trade controls of the 1930s at a time when the dollar payments problem looked so severe an open 'line of credit' on favourable terms of $3,750 million (£931 million) was established in Washington, plus a loan on similar terms to pay for the Lend-Lease goods 'in the pipeline'.

There was opposition from both right and left to the acceptance of these terms, chiefly on the grounds that the full employment policy as well as the various social and economic reforms which accompanied it would be made impossible if the British economy were tied by a convertible currency in a multilateral trade system at a time when the dollar was so preponderant to the notoriously volatile economy of the United States, whose social and economic objectives might prove different. The opponents of the American loan asserted that this was the final loss of any worthwhile scope for independent *domestic* economic action in Britain. They would, for the most part, have agreed with Parker about the earlier consequences for Britain's international autonomy, in as much as although for four and a half years Lend-Lease, financial ingenuity and accumulated wealth had allowed the United Kingdom to play the role of a great military power, the dollar loan marked the ultimate triumph of American policy.

In the event things turned out quite differently. The Bretton Woods multilateral payments system collapsed completely in 1947 only six weeks after the British government had honoured the Financial Agreements and made the pound convertible against the dollar. By that time the 'line of credit' was already almost exhausted. The powerful surge of investment in all western European economies doubled the size of western Europe's dollar deficits in 1947 compared to those of 1946 and Britain itself was more responsible for the increase than others. At the same time as American plans for post-war international reconstruction collapsed America's strategic interests in the emerging cold war demanded that western Europe be strengthened economically and reconstructed politically as a defence against the Soviet Union, even if this meant postponing a further attempt to establish the principles agreed at Bretton Woods. The outcome was the European Recovery Programme (The Marshall Plan) which concentrated the outflow of dollars from the United States economy on to western Europe while allowing western European economies, including Britain, to continue to expand while discriminating in trade and payments against the dollar.

In effect the Marshall Plan backed up the expansionist programmes of the British and other western European economies while absolving Britain from most of the international obligations it had reluctantly accepted from 1938 onwards as the price of American support and which might in other circumstances have slowed down economic expansion. The price for this change of policy was that Britain should take

71

the lead in creating an 'integrated' western Europe, but since that never happened and, indeed, was expressly renounced at the time of the devaluation of the pound in 1949, that price was not paid either. The chance of history meant a radical change in the policy the United States had pursued since 1938 and meant also that Britain had fresh room for autonomous policies. Parker's arguments must be seen in this wider perspective, wherein they appear as marked exaggerations. Yet they do focus on a question of central importance. In the Second World War as in the First the problem of international adjustment to the extraordinarily rapid changes in the relative positions of Britain and the United States was a severe one and dominated in each case the immediate post-war world, raising the most profound questions about the future of the British economy and society. That a nation still considered a great power in 1913 and which, indeed, again functioned as a major military force in the world between 1940 and 1945, should in so short a space of time afterwards have to question so fundamentally the terms on which it might survive into the future is a powerful testimony to the scope of the effects of the world wars on the world as a whole.

The domestic economic and social changes in Britain which the war produced were only durable in so far as the international situation of the United Kingdom continued to permit large surpluses of imports over exports while also allowing for a continued increase in wealth. This remained true in spite of the perceptible change in the commodity composition of British manufacturing output and exports in the first five years after the Second World War compared to the five years before it, as well as the remarkable, roughly 75 per cent, increase in the total value of exports over the same period. The manufacturing experience of the Second World War did increase the proportion of capital goods and machinery in British industrial output and exports compared to textiles and other consumer products. Again, however, the questions are how durable these changes were and whether they went far enough. In practice the balance of payments problems remained acute, more so than those of other western European economies of a similar size and over the post-war period as a whole they worsened. It may be that the tendency of British manufactures to be exported to softer non-European markets after the war mitigated against the changes in productivity and commodity composition which the war may have brought about. Although the contribution of income from foreign investments to paying for the import surplus was much lower in the immediate aftermath of the Second World War, British foreign investment very soon resumed and has remained at a high level since, although not at the pre-1914 levels, so that the cause of these endemic balance of payments problems does not lie there. The evidence repeatedly suggests that in booms Britain's imports are comparatively greater than economies of similar size and structure and that the import content of British exports is higher. While trade controls and trade discrimination persisted these problems were held in check, although at the time many politicians and economists argued that they nevertheless held back the rate of growth of national income compared to other European economies. After 1958, when there was a return to a world-wide multilateral payments system and when foreign trade restrictions were for a while genuinely removed on a more impressive scale, the balance of payments problems became noticeably worse and there is everything to indicate that once the fortuitous effects of the discovery of the North Sea oil fields are no longer there they will be worse still.

If the world wars did induce in the British economy the domestic economic changes ascribed to them here, did they in doing so increase the weakness of Britain's international position, or is that to be attributed to other causes which may, in fact, have been partly mitigated by the wars? It is now alleged loudly that the Welfare State increased the level of internal costs in the economy and made successful inter-national competition more difficult and, in some only vaguely specified way, lowered the level of initiative and dynamism in the economy. The party which is currently in power with a large majority specifically wishes for these reasons to undo many of the changes which to most historians even ten years ago appeared as an irreversible long-term trend. By contrast, fifteen years ago, when the first edition of this pamphlet was conceived, the existence of counter-cyclical employment policies and the Welfare State was most frequently given as a cause for the unprecedented prosperity and stability of west European economies. The domestic changes engendered by the two world wars have thus in one decade passed from being considered a substantial advantage to the workings of the international capitalist economy to being considered, in Britain at least, as a severe handicap to the country's capacity to survive in that economy.

That this could be the case in itself testifies to the serious and accelerating deterioration in Britain's international position of which the first symptoms became publicly evident in 1915. Although the composition of manufacturing output was changed by both wars, the changes were not such as fundamentally to change the composition or direction of British foreign trade or to offer a better solution to the problem of paying for imports. By their impact elsewhere, especially in the United States, the wars compressed into a short space of time what might have been a much longer drawn out process of the relative diminution of Britain's international economic importance. This problem was always most evident with respect to the relative positions of the United Kingdom and the United States, but there were equally sudden adjustments in economic relationships with less mighty nations. In posing these sudden adjustment problems (which were not solved) the world wars called into question, at the least, the durability of those very domestic economic and social benefits which they had brought to Britain. At the extreme of the argument, by promoting false benefits they may have eliminated all hope of successfully making the necessary international adjustment. It is on finding the correct point on the scale of this argument that historical discussion is likely to be concentrated in the future.

Another constantly underlying theme of the general election of 1983 was the implicit questioning as to whether the United Kingdom had made correct choices in opting after the last war for a multilateral payments system rather than choosing to persist with trade discrimination: the same questions were asked about the later option for the European Economic Community. Opponents of the American loan in 1945, like opponents of the EEC, were divided amongst themselves and

74

subject to the reproach made by Keynes in 1944 that they were advocating for a long time into the future 'a siege economy'. They also had to face the reality that what they were advocating was tantamount to a reversal of the whole path of the United Kingdom's modern economic development, a reversal which perhaps now seems to some a more justifiable risk. During the great boom of the post-war years argument was stilled, re-emerging only in the 1960s when it became clear that Britain's performance in the great boom had not been as impressive as that of other European countries. With the end of the great boom and the return of violent depressive movements in the economy, accompanied by cruelly high unemployment and the stagnation of real income growth, many politicians and some economists who wish above all to retain the domestic changes which have been analysed here now advocate a return to trade and exchange controls and protection. Another war would not, presumably, solve the problem. As the once seemingly irreversible social and economic trends which the two wars produced in Britain continue to be reversed the question as to whether the international economic choices made after the wars by Britain properly took account of the whole impact of the wars on Britain and the world will increasingly be posed. For it was on those choices that the future welfare, the future survival indeed, of the very large number of people in this old, complex and now increasingly divided society depended.

The liberal interpretation of war has been wholly discredited and discarded but its great advantage lay in its universality. Only when the debate on the effect of the wars on this country is widened to acknowledge the interaction of the rest of the world with Britain and the impact of the war outside these islands will a more satisfactory, but equally universal, interpretation be produced. The trends of economic and social change in Britain may in the long run prove to be as much explained by the impact of the world wars on the rest of the world as by their impact on British society alone.

Notes and References

Unless otherwise indicated, London is the place of publication.

1. That there is general agreement on these matters can be seen by comparing the accounts of the Second World War in S. Pollard, *The Development of the British Economy 1914–1967* (1969) and A. J. Youngson, *Britain's Economic Growth 1920–1966* (1967), books written from different political standpoints. W. Ashworth, *An Economic History of England, 1870–1939* (1960) and Pollard both have clear and comprehensive accounts of the First World War.

2. It was a completely eighteenth-century gloss on what Juvenal had written, which is more nearly rendered in Dryden's translation:

> Of every nation, each illustrious name,
> Such toys as those have cheated into fame;
> Exchanging solid quiet, to obtain
> The windy satisfaction of the brain.

3. The origins of the idea are found in Sir R. Giffen, *Economic Inquiries and Studies* (1904), pp. 1–74, where the author attempted something similar for the Boer War. But there the numbers involved were smaller and the 'human capital' more homogeneous.

4. The values were taken from calculations by a French actuary, P. Barriol, published in *Revue Economique Internationale* (December 1910 and May 1911).

5. Whether these elements were all real costs or merely transfer payments was never considered.

6. G. Jèze, *Les Dépenses de guerre de la France* (Paris, 1926).

7. A. Smith, *The Wealth of Nations* (Edinburgh, 1776).

8. United Kingdom, Ministry of Health, *On the State of the Public Health During Six Years of War* (1946).

9. Sir W. Beveridge, *Social Insurance and Allied Services*, in *Parliamentary Papers*, 1942–3, VI.

10. E. F. Nash, 'Wartime Control of Food and Agricultural Prices', in National Institute of Economic and Social Research, *Lessons of the British War Economy* (Cambridge, 1951).

11. In this respect there are some interesting calculations in Sir G. Ince, 'The Mobilization of Manpower in Great Britain for the Second World War', in *Manchester School of Social and Economic Studies*, XIV (1946).

12. The same effects were produced in the United States in spite of the greater level of mechanisation of industry. A. F. Hinrichs, 'The Defence Program and Labor Supply in the United States', *Canadian Journal of Economics and Political Science*, VII (1941).

13. The most typical and the standard for many other such surveys was B. Seebohm Rowntree, *Poverty: A Study of Town Life* (1901).

14. Rowntree surveyed the same population, York, in 1935 as a control, a convincing demonstration. B. Seebohm Rowntree, *Poverty and Progress. A Second Social Survey of York* (1935).

15. Rowntree tried again in a much slighter work, B. Seebohm Rowntree and G. R. Lavers, *Poverty and the Welfare State* (1951). But it was undertaken too early to answer these questions.

16. *Report of the Committee on National Debt and Taxation, Parliamentary Papers*, 1927, XI.

17. *Report of the Committee of the Privy Council for Scientific and Industrial Research for the year 1915–16*, p. 42, *Parliamentary Papers*, 1916, VIII.

18. Ministry of Reconstruction Pamphlets, no. 23.

19. *Parliamentary Papers*, 1905, XXXIV.

20. J. H. Kirk, *Agriculture and the Trade Cycle, 1926–1931* (1933).

21. *Final Report of the Committee on Industry and Trade, Parliamentary Papers*, 1928–29, VII.

22. United Nations, *The European Economy in 1947* (Geneva, 1948).

23. For detailed calculations to support these assertions see the author's forthcoming, *The Reconstruction of Western Europe, 1945–1952* (1984).

24. *Statistical Material Presented During the Washington Negotiations*, Cmnd. 6707.

25. Sir R. Clarke, *Anglo-American Economic Collaboration in War and Peace, 1942–1949* (ed. Sir A. Cairncross, Oxford, 1982).

Select Bibliography

The Carnegie Endowment for International Peace, Division of Economics and History, began during the course of the First World War to commission certain studies on the economic and social history of that war. At the end of the war this developed into a plan for commissioning a complete economic and social history of the war for all the nations involved. This ambitious scheme petered out in the 1930s. The books which were produced under its aegis are, effectively, individual monographs rather than part of a general work. They are like other books, some good, some bad and some awful. Books which are in this series are indicated with an asterisk (*).

The Cabinet Office Historical Section undertook a similar task for Britain after the Second World War. In this case all the volumes are part of a common plan and all have a common stamp. They are the records of ministerial policy written by independent authors. All, without exception, therefore, irrespective of their quality as books, have a particular and special usefulness. I have indicated here only those which are immediately relevant to the themes touched on in this pamphlet; but no disrespect is meant to the authors of those omitted. Books in this series (History of the Second World War, United Kingdom Civil Series) are indicated with a dagger (†).

[1] P. Abrams, 'The Failure of Social Reform, 1918–1920', *Past and Present*, no. 24 (1963). Argues that the ability of particular social groups to benefit from war depends on the degree to which they participate, which varies widely, and on their power to influence political decisions. He takes the view that previous theories about war and social change, in particular that of Andrzejewski, have been too undiscriminating.

[2] *I. O. Andrews, *Economic Effects of the War upon Women and Children in Great Britain* (New York, 1918). For all its brevity, the best book on its subject.

[3] S. Andrzejewski, *Military Organisation and Society* (1954). Proposes the theory of the 'military participation ratio', that there is in every society an optimum ratio of military participation in

war and that the gap between that optimum ratio and the actual ratio enables us to see which social groups will benefit in future wars by becoming involved.

[4] *Sir W. H. Beveridge, *British Food Control* (1928). Has much wider importance than its title suggests. It is indispensable for its information on consumption levels during and after the war and is also interesting because of the role its author subsequently played.

[5] *E. L. Bogart, *Direct Costs of the Present War* (New York, 1918). Is a preliminary study for [6].

[6] *————, *Direct and Indirect Costs of the Great World War* (1920). The most complete attempt actually to calculate the financial cost of all aspects of the war within the terms of classical liberal theory. Although Bogart draws heavily on statistical procedures and methodological concepts first employed by others the comprehensiveness of his work is such as to make it represent the culminating point of a whole approach to the subject.

[7] *A. L. Bowley, *Prices and Wages in the United Kingdom, 1914–20* (1921). The best attempt at measuring the true movement and distribution of real wage rates and earnings in its period.

[8] ————, *Some Economic Consequences of the Great War* (1930) is a summation of much earlier published work and touches on almost all the themes which had interested Bowley. His approach is fiercely statistical, but his thoroughness and his determination to measure everything that could be measured has made his work the starting-point of much subsequent discussion which is neither as thorough nor as cautious.

[9] R. H. Brand, *War and National Finance* (1921). A series of essays published throughout the war by an international financier who was able to view the situation both with the involvement of a businessman and the detachment of an Oxford Fellow. A resolutely liberal approach; only in the very last essay does he perceive the social change which the war brought about.

[10] G. Braybon, *Women Workers in the First World War. The British Experience* (1981). Argues convincingly that very little long-run change in the position of women in the economy arose out of the First World War.

[11] K. Burk, 'J. M. Keynes and the Exchange Rate Crisis of July 1917', *Economic History Review*, XXXII, 3, 1979.

[12] ————, 'Great Britain and the United States, 1917–1918: The Turning Point', *International History Review*, I, 2, 1979. Argues that the inability of the United Kingdom to sustain the exchange

rate of sterling against the dollar in those years marked the replacement of Britain by the United States as the leading power on world financial markets.

[13] ———, (ed.), *War and the State. The Transformation of British Government, 1914–1919* (1982). A collection of essays illustrating the impact of the war on governmental and administrative practice.

[14] *G. D. H. Cole, *Trade Unionism and Munitions* (1923). A study of the impact of mechanisation on the trade union movement and, occasionally, on the workers.

[15] †W. H. B. Court, *Coal* (1951). An excellent study of an industry which failed to improve either its production or its productivity in wartime.

[16] G. A. B. Dewar, *The Great Munitions Feat, 1914–18* (1941). Not intended as a scholarly study, but a very good summary of what actually happened in wartime factories.

[17] N. F. Dreisziger (ed.), *Mobilization for Total War. The Canadian, American and British Experience 1914–1918, 1939–1945* (Waterloo, Ontario, 1981). Contains the most recent and concise statement of Marwick's hypothesis and an interesting article by Burk.

[18] *S. Dumas and K. O. Vedel-Petersen, *Losses of Life Caused by War*, Part II: *The World War* (1923).

[19] H. Durant and J. Goldmann, 'The Distribution of Working-Class Savings', *Bulletin of the Oxford University Institute of Statistics*, VII (1945). Shows how unequal their distribution was and how low they were.

[20] R. Easterlin, *The Postwar American Baby Boom in Historical Perspective*, National Bureau of Economic Research, Occasional Paper 79 (Princeton, 1962). Shows the impact of the end of the war on the American birth-rate and raises many intriguing questions about the demographic impact of wars generally.

[21] *C. E. Fayle, *The War and the Shipping Industry* (1927). Makes a useful factual contribution to the debate on the relationship of the First World War to the following depression.

[22] A. W. Flux, 'Our Food Supply before and after the War', *Journal of the Royal Statistical Society*, LXXXX (1930). Shows the changes in agricultural production and diet which were furthered by the First World War.

[23] W. H. Form and C. P. Loomis, 'The Persistence and Emergence of Social and Cultural Systems in Disasters', *American Sociological Review*, XXI (1956). See also [24].

[24] ———, and S. Nosow, *Community in Disaster* (New York, 1958). Shows the deep resistance to cultural and economic change which 'disaster' can produce, together with its tendency to accelerate such changes.

[25] D. French, *British Economic and Strategic Planning 1905–1915* (1982). One of the few studies of the First World War with a wide enough definition of strategy to do justice to its subject.

[26] M. Gowing, *Britain and Atomic Energy 1939–1945* (1964). An official account of what turned out to be the most important of the wartime research and development projects.

[27] †H. D. Hall, *North American Supply* (1955). Important for the international effects of the Second World War.

[28] †———, and C. C. Wrigley, *Studies of Overseas Supply* (1956). See [27] above.

[29] †W. K. Hancock and M. M. Gowing, *The British War Economy* (1949). A most successful attempt to summarise the important themes of the other official histories, although at times rather bland.

[30] J. Harris, *William Beveridge* (Oxford, 1977). A biography with occasional interesting sidelights on the war.

[31] *B. H. Hibbard, *Effects of the Great War upon Agriculture in the United States and Great Britain* (New York, 1919). A useful factual study.

[32] *F. W. Hirst and J. E. Allen, *British War Budgets* (1928). An angry liberal denunciation of government policy and its harmful effects.

[33] *F. W. Hirst, *The Consequences of the War to Great Britain* (1934). Hirst turned what should have been the summary volume in the Carnegie Series into a passionate statement of his own views which were by that time becoming discredited.

[34] †W. Hornby, *Factories and Plant* (1958). Shows the scale of production and organisation required in the Second World War.

[35] S. J. Hurwitz, *State Intervention in Great Britain, 1914–18* (New York, 1949). Very much a study of opinion.

[36] P. B. Johnson, *Land Fit for Heroes. The Planning of British Reconstruction, 1916–19* (Chicago, 1968). From which we also see how limited the long-run change wrought by the First World War was.

[37] J. M. Keynes, *The Economic Consequences of the Peace* (1920). A study of the probable effects of the peace treaty on the international economy.

[38] ———, *How to Pay for the War* (1940). Originally published as a series of articles in *The Times*, this essay contains the author's proposals for deferred pay.

[39] A. W. Kirkaldy (ed.), *British Finance, during and after the War, 1914–21* (1921). One of the first and sternest criticisms of financial policy in the First World War.

[40] K. Langley, 'The Distribution of Capital in Private Hands in 1936–8 and 1946–7', *Bulletin of the Oxford University Institute of Statistics*, XIII (1951).

[41] C. E. V. Leser, 'Changes in the Level and Diversity of Employment in Regions of Great Britain, 1939–1947', *Economic Journal*, LIX (1949).

[42] *E. M. H. Lloyd, *Experiments in State Control* (1924). While describing excellently the slow process by which the government was drawn into economic life in the First World War, Lloyd also used those events as a parable to preach in a most spirited way his own views on economic management and 'efficiency'. The most interesting and provocative of all the Carnegie histories, marking a turning-point in the interpretation of the war.

[43] A. M. Low, *Benefits of War* (1943). The title speaks for itself.

[44] D. F. McCurrach, 'Britain's U.S. Dollar Problem, 1939–45', *Economic Journal*, LVIII (1948). A statement of the movement and size of the dollar debt during the Second World War.

[45] A. Marwick, *The Deluge* (1965). The first general statement of Marwick's hypothesis on war and social change.

[46] ———, *Britain in the Century of Total War* (1968). A similar but briefer survey.

[47] ———, *War and Social Change in the Twentieth Century. A Comparative Study of Britain, France, Germany, Russia and the United States* (1974). Looks at social change in a less strictly economic perspective than in this book and explores the relationships between psychological and social change during and after the world wars.

[48] ———, *The Home Front: The British and the Second World War* (1976).

[49] ———, *Women at War, 1914–1918* (1977).

[50] R. C. O. Matthews, C. H. Feinstein and J. C. Odling-Smee, *British Economic Growth, 1856–1973* (Oxford, 1982).

[51] A. S. Milward, *War, Economy and Society 1939–1945* (1977). Attempts to define a wide range of general relationships between war and economy by examining the experience of all the major combatants in the Second World War.

82

[52] E. V. Morgan, *Studies in British Financial Policy, 1914–25* (1952). The clearest exposition of that policy.

[53] †K. A. H. Murray, *Agriculture* (1955). A clear account of the changes in British agriculture during the Second World War, prefaced by an exposition of previous trends.

[54] National Institute of Economic and Social Research, *Lessons of the British War Economy* (Cambridge, 1951). A series of essays on the day-to-day administrative functioning of, and changes in, the economic administration during the Second World War.

[55] J. L. Nicholson, 'Employment and National Income during the War', *Bulletin of the Oxford University Institute of Statistics*, VII (1945).

[56] ———, 'Earnings and Hours of Labour, 1938–1945', *Bulletin of the Oxford University Institute of Statistics*, VIII (1946). Nicholson's articles contain a comprehensive examination of the official 'cost-of-living' index.

[57] R. A. C. Parker, 'The Pound Sterling, the American Treasury and British Preparations for War, 1938–1939', *English Historical Review*, XCVIII (1983). Argues that the failure of the American Treasury to support the pound on the foreign exchanges in these two years effectively marked the end of British economic independence.

[58] †M. M. Postan, *British War Production* (1952). One of the more revealing of the official histories which is also an excellent summary of subjects handled in other volumes.

[59] †R. S. Sayers, *Financial Policy, 1939–45* (1956). An excellent study which reveals the essential continuity of government policy and the extent to which that policy had already been permeated by 'Keynesian' ideas before the war even though those ideas had had less effect on the Treasury.

[60] D. Seers, *Changes in the Cost of Living and the Distribution of Income since 1938* (Oxford, 1949). A collection of the author's articles in the *Bulletin of the Oxford University Institute of Statistics*, constituting the best attempt at actually measuring the social changes brought about by the war since Bowley's attempts to do the same thing for the First World War.

[61] R. P. Shay (Jr.), *British Rearmament in the Thirties. Politics and Profits* (Princeton, 1977). A useful documentary study of the government's fear of the economic disruptions of rearmament.

[62] P. A. Sorokin, *Man and Society in Calamity* (New York, 1942). The starting-point of much subsequent research on this topic.

[63] Sir J. Stamp, *The Financial Aftermath of War* (1932). Is useful for

its consideration of the changes which the First World War brought in the taxation system.

[64] R. H. Tawney, 'The Abolition of Economic Controls, 1918–1921', *Economic History Review*, XIII (1943). Tawney regarded their abolition as inevitable but unwise, since it was against the long-run trend of the economy, which he regarded as desirable. A fuller version is in [68].

[65] †R. M. Titmuss, *Problems of Social Policy* (1950). A most instructive book on war. It is here that the author's theories on the social results of the Second World War are most fully set out.

[66] ———, *Essays on the 'Welfare State'* (1958). Two of the essays discuss Titmuss's view of the relationship between war and social change, the theme which binds all the essays together.

[67] M. Van Creveld, *Supplying War. Logistics from Wallenstein to Patton* (Cambridge, 1977). A highly interesting book about the economic consequences of particular military tactics.

[68] J. M. Winter (ed.), *War and Economic Development. Essays in Memory of David Joslin* (Cambridge, 1975). Its title itself shows the change in concepts which had taken place by that date. There are several apposite essays.

[69] ———, (ed.), *History and Society: Essays by R. H. Tawney* (1978). Contains a fuller version of [64].

[70] ———, 'Aspects of the Impact of the First World War on Infant Mortality in Britain', *Journal of European Economic History*, XI, 3, (1982). One of the first serious demographic studies of the consequences of the war and one with far-reaching conclusions.

[71] *H. Wolfe, *Labour Supply and Regulation* (1923). A useful study of the changes in the labour market in the First World War.

Index

85